Informed REITs Investing

A Beginner's Guide to Understanding Real Estate Investment Trusts

Michael Allard

Table of Contents

Foreword/Introduction

A long, long time ago – back when I was just a kid fresh out of college, thrilled and mesmerized by the flashy spectacle that was my first job in Wall Street – one of the many mentors I would end up having impact my life told me this: Investing isn't about taking risks. It's about management – of expectations, of knowledge and, of course, of assets. Up until that point, even with my fancy degree, investing was a gamble. An educated one, sure, but still just a bet in favor or against the odds. This guy made me understand that investing is only a gamble if you don't do the homework. "That's what we offer our clients," he explained. "Not the act of making the acquisition, but the advice and expertise necessary to educate them so they know how and when to buy."

I took that lesson with me through that first job, and my second, and my third, and along with me when I opened up my own consultancy (which I've since sold, as part of one of those educated decisions I just mentioned). The reason I bring that up is because I know not everyone feels the same my mentor did, and I still do, about helping people make the best decisions. Nowadays, it seems it's all about cold service, with no real dedication and care for the people that seeking assistance. And that's what this book is. No more, no less.

REITs have proven a wise investment for me over these recent years and I know there are others out there for whom it can do the same. Maybe that's not you, dear reader, or maybe it is. My job now, with this book, is to educate about what real estate investment trusts are, why they might be worth it for you, and how best to optimize returns. Your task, once you finish reading, will be to decide if you want to follow through. REITs are a great opportunity for investors, large and small. I do believe that. They are a kind of company that owns and, in the majority of cases, manages real estate holdings that generate revenue for the company. This also comes with a series of added benefits that change from country to country, such as tax incentives. Which is why it's important that you do your own local research if you decide to proceed.

In fact, just to illustrate why location matters, I should note that, in the case of the US, for example, it was Congress that came up with the concept of REITs to make it possible for average citizens to buy real estate. Before the framework was put in place, individuals who had a considerable amount of money were the only ones who could participate in the game. Now, however, the playing field is more level for everyone. Now it can be as easy as just a few clicks of a mouse by almost anybody who has a brokerage account, some spare cash, and internet connection.

Look, I don't have a magic ball. I don't need one. I can tell you this, though: In this book, I will lay it all down for you, every piece of information that you need to make the best possible decisions. I'm not here to convince you of anything, just to educate you. Because I believe REITs are worth it, but only if you learn the trades first.

Education will be our friend in this journey, because it's with information that we turn blind bets into informed decisions. If you're looking for a quick, easy buck, might be best to look somewhere else. If not, I'm glad you're here, with me, in this road. Together, we'll turn risks into opportunities, and, hopefully, you'll feel empowered and informed enough to seek out your fortune.

Enjoy.

-Michael Allard

Chapter 1

Real Estate Investment Trusts

A REIT is a kind of organization that owns and, in the majority of instances, manages income-generating real estate properties. REITs can acquire a diverse portfolio of commercial real estate, including office and apartment buildings, storage facilities, hospitals, retail complexes, hotels, and commercial forests. Some REITs are also involved in the real estate finance industry.

They were created back in the 60s by the Eienhower administration as part of an effort to give all types of investors to invest in diversified portfolios of income-producing real estate, much in the same way as they might in other classes of assets. This matters, because the regulations governing REITs in most nations allow real estate companies to pay lower rates of corporation tax and capital gains tax, not to mention the fact that they have the potential to be either publicly traded on major markets, publicly registered but unlisted, or even stay private.

Equity REITs and mortgage REITs are the two primary categories of real estate investment trusts. In the Global Industry Classification Standard that was released by S&P Dow Jones Indices and MSCI in November 2014, equity REITs were acknowledged as a separate asset class for the first time. The net asset value (NAV), funds from operations (FFO), and adjusted funds from operations are the most important metrics to consider when analyzing the financial status and activities of a REIT (AFFO).

All these terms might seem daunting now, but it'll all become clearer as we delve deeper and explore the various benefits of REITs. That said, they are not without detractors. REITs have been the target of criticism for how they enable speculation on housing and decrease housing affordability while not boosting financing for development. This, too, we will explore to better balance the information.

1.1   What does REIT stand for?

Real Estate Investment Trust is what "REIT" stands for in the industry. A real estate investment trust (REIT) is a partnership, company, trust, or association that invests directly in real estate by purchasing properties or mortgages. REITs may be established as either a corporation or a trust. Shares of a REIT are issued, traded on the stock market, and purchased and sold in the same manner as regular equities. A corporation must invest at least 75% of its total assets in real estate and generate at least 75% of its total revenues from real estate-related operations to qualify as a real estate investment trust, often known as a REIT.

1.2   What makes a REIT unique

In 1960, the Congress decided to create REITs to provide investors of all sizes, but notably smaller investors, with access to income-generating real estate. Since that time, the method used in the United States for real estate investment trusts (REITs) has grown and been used as a model in around 40 nations across the globe. On September 14, 1960, President Dwight D. Eisenhower signed legislation that established a new method for investing in real estate to earn income. This method combines the positive aspects of investing in real estate and stock-based investments in a single strategy. Before the creation of REITs, the advantages of investing in commercial real estate were previously only accessible to rich people and major financial intermediaries. REITs made it possible for average Americans to participate in the market for commercial real estate for the first time. The Tax Reform Act of 1986 laid the framework for the Modern REIT Era by granting REITs the capacity to run and manage real estate in addition to merely owning or financing it. This ability to operate and manage real estate expanded the scope of what a REIT might do. Today, nearly 145 million Americans reside in the approximately 43% of American households that own REIT equities, either directly or indirectly via mutual funds, ETFs, or target date funds. These households account for a total of around $2.1 trillion in assets under management.

REITs have also gained popularity on a global scale, and as of today, 40 countries around the world, including all of the nations that make up the Group of Seven (G-7) and almost two-thirds of the countries that make up the Organization for Economic Co-operation and Development (OECD), have a REIT regime in place. Investing opportunities in income-generating real estate are now available to investors from all over the globe.

Additionally, the REIT business is continuously changing to become a more varied and welcoming place of employment. This shift has resulted in an increase in the number of women working in the industry as well as a diversification of board members. As we go farther down this road, NAREIT will continue to uphold its commitment to the Dividends through Diversity & Inclusion (DDI) Initiative, through which it will educate and enlighten its members about the most pressing challenges facing our industry.

1.3   How REITs Work

In 1960, as part of an amendment to the Cigar Excise Tax Extension, the United States Congress formed REITs. The provision makes it possible for investors to own shares in commercial real estate portfolios, which was a possibility that was previously restricted to affluent people and huge financial intermediaries.

Apartment complexes, data centers, healthcare facilities, hotels, infrastructure (in the form of fiber cables, cell towers, and energy pipelines), office buildings, retail centers, self-storage, timberland, and warehouses are some examples of the types of properties that may be included in the portfolio of a REIT. In general, REITs concentrate in a single real estate industry. However, diversified and specialty REITs may include a variety of property kinds within their portfolios. One example of this would be a REIT that is comprised of both office and retail buildings. During the trading session, investors can purchase and sell a variety of REITs much like stocks since a large number of REITs are traded publicly on major securities exchanges. These REITs generally trade under large volume and are regarded as particularly liquid products due to their high level of liquidity.

1.3.1 Typical REIT Structure

- The REIT conducts an initial public offering (IPO) to collect capital from its unit holders; this capital is then utilized by the REIT to buy a portfolio of real estate assets.
- Tenants are subsequently given leases on these buildings to occupy them.
- In exchange, the revenue is distributed as income distributions to the investors who own units in the investment vehicle (which are similar to dividends)
- The majority of real estate investment trusts (REITs) have yearly expenditures such as REIT managers' fees, property manager's fees, trustees' fees, and other charges, all of which are taken from their earnings before distributions are given.
- There is a possibility that some REITs that have holdings in properties located in several countries will also be liable to taxes in those countries. Both the REITs' prospectuses and their financial statements provide information that investors may utilize to learn more about these fees.

1.4 Types of REITs

There are three different kinds of real estate investment trusts (REITs):

- **Equity REITs.** REITs that are owned by investors. The majority of REITs are equity REITs, which own and operate real estate that generates income for their shareholders. Rents are the primary contributor to the company's revenue (not by reselling properties).

- **Mortgage REITs**. Mortgage real estate investment trusts (REITs) lend money to owners and operators of real estate either directly through mortgages and loans or indirectly through the purchase of mortgage-backed securities. Mortgages and loans fall under the "direct" category. The net interest margin represents the spread between the interest they earn on mortgage loans and the cost of funding these loans. This margin is the primary driver of their profits. It is the difference between the two. Because of this model, they are potentially vulnerable to increases in the interest rate.
- **Hybrid REITs**. These REITs invest in a combination of equity and mortgage REITs, using their respective investing techniques.
- **Publicly Traded REITs**. Real Estate Investment Trusts That Are Traded Publicly. Individual investors are the ones who buy and sell the shares of publicly traded real estate investment trusts (REITs), which are listed on a national securities exchange. The United States Securities and Exchange Commission is in charge of their oversight (SEC).
- **Public Non-Traded REITs**. Publicly Held Real Estate Investment Trusts. These real estate investment trusts (REITs) are likewise registered with the SEC, but their shares are not traded on any major securities exchanges. As a direct consequence of this, their liquidity is lower than that of publicly listed REITs. 5 However, since

they are not affected by changes in the market, they have a greater propensity to be more stable.

- **Private REITs**. These real estate investment trusts are neither registered with the Securities and Exchange Commission (SEC), nor do they trade on any national securities exchanges. In most cases, private real estate investment trusts (REITs) may be sold to only institutional investors.

1.4.1 Market Type

It is also possible to classify REITs according to the market on which they are traded, which, in the end, affects the means through which investors may have access to them. This difference is very important for individual investors, given that a REIT's market may influence both who is allowed to access it and the minimum amount that can be invested in it. First, real estate investment trusts are often classified according to two factors: first, whether or not they are regulated by the Securities and Exchange Commission (SEC), and second, whether or not their shares are listed on an exchange.

- Similar to how publicly traded firm shares are registered with the SEC and published on a public stock market, publicly traded real estate investment trusts (REITs) are also subject to these same requirements.
- Private REITs are not needed to register with the SEC and are not required to be listed on an exchange to participate in trading.
- Public non-traded REITs are required to be registered with the SEC, but they are not required to be listed on a

public exchange. In addition, you could hear people refer to them as non-listed REITs. (As will be shown in the next section, Fundrise's eREITs are one-of-a-kind investments that do not fit into any of the conventional REIT categories. However, their operations are most analogous to those of public REITs that are not traded.)

1.4.2   Publicly Traded REITs

Investors may reap the advantages of SEC regulation, public reporting, and open trading on a public exchange with publicly listed real estate investment trusts (REITs). Investors have a simple and convenient method to get access to liquid assets when they trade on a stock exchange, and there is no required minimum holding time. The ability to access daily liquidity does, however, come with an inherent cost that is referred to as the "liquidity premium," which reduces the earning potential of an investment.

Because liquidity is such a prevalent characteristic of the stock market, many investors automatically prioritize it as a priority. However, paying a "liquidity premium" is not always in the best interest of an investor. This is particularly true if the investor is seeking long-term growth in an environment with low trading, such as when establishing savings accounts for retirement. ETFs provide investors with another another public and liquid option for investing in REITs (exchange traded funds). REIT exchange-traded funds, like the Vanguard REIT ETF, are single publicly listed funds that invest in several public REITs simultaneously. Similar to the assets that are held by an index fund, REIT exchange-traded funds (ETFs) make it possible to invest in many public REITs via a single, diversified offering.

The fact that the performance of publicly listed REITs is significantly connected to that of the overall public market is perhaps the most significant disadvantage associated with these investments. Because of this connection, there is volatility, and as a result, share values tend to go up and down in unison with the overall movement of the stock market. This is something that may take place regardless of whether or not there have been any significant changes to the underlying properties that are held by the REIT.

Because of this correlation with public markets, publicly traded REITs do not offer much in the way of true diversification beyond the typical assets found in public markets. True diversification is something that is typically anticipated when making an investment in a new asset class such as real estate.

1.4.3 Private REITs

Private real estate investment trusts are not required to register with the Securities and Exchange Commission (SEC) and are not traded on any exchanges. Private real estate investment trusts often provide a limited level of liquidity since they are not listed on any public exchanges. On the other hand, because of this characteristic, their success is not associated with the performance of the stock market. Because of this, private REITs have the potential to provide substantial asset class diversity and act as a viable alternative investment option.

Private REITs are only accessible to accredited individual investors and institutional investors since they are not registered with the SEC and they are not listed on an exchange. By the laws, private REITs may only be purchased by these two types of investors. In addition, they often have larger minimum investment levels, in addition to hefty fees, both of which might be prohibitive for many investors who are qualified to contribute but choose not to.

1.4.4 Public Non-Traded REITs

Non-traded real estate investment trusts, also known as non-listed REITs, have recently gained in popularity because they can provide wider access to investors, in large part because of the JOBS Act of 2012; they also have the potential to diversify their holdings, and the historical performance of some non-traded REITs has consistently delivered double-digit returns to investors. Because the SEC oversees public non-traded REITs, the regulations that govern them are quite similar to those that control typical public REITs. This indicates that they provide a significant amount of openness, which includes public reporting. Non-traded REITs, on the other hand, do not provide its shareholders the option of selling their shares on a secondary market since they are not listed on a public exchange. As a result, non-traded REITs have a lower level of liquidity. Start your real estate investment portfolio with as little as ten dollars.

However, similar to a private REIT, the performance of a non-traded REIT is not tied to the performance (and, therefore, the volatility) of a public market investment. This is because non-traded REITs are not publicly listed. Because of these qualities, public non-traded REITs are a valid choice as an "alternative investment," which allows you to diversify your investment portfolio by include a new asset class. This is the case for private REITs as well. It is essential to be aware that, similar to a private REIT, the accessibility and investment minimum of public non-traded REITs might differ from REIT to REIT. This is because public non-traded REITs aren't offered or traded on an exchange.

1.4.5 Focus of Sector

One such way to classify equity REITs is according to the different kinds of real estate in which they invest. This is where different REIT strategies truly can vary from one another. There is a diverse and extensive selection of REIT sectors accessible to choose from. There are real estate investment trusts (REITs) that concentrate on every conceivable kind of property, including apartment complexes, data centers, and self-storage facilities. There are other types of REITs, such as healthcare REITs that concentrate on medical assets, residential REITs that concentrate on residential buildings, retail REITs that concentrate on shopping, and so on. If there is a certain kind of property that you are interested in owning, there is a good possibility that there is a real estate investment trust (REIT) that specializes in that particular form of real estate.

1.5 What Qualifies as a REIT?

The majority of real estate investment trusts (REITs) operate under a rather simple business model. This strategy entails the REIT leasing out space, collecting rents on the buildings it owns, and then distributing that money to its shareholders in the form of dividends. Mortgage REITs don't own any property; rather, they provide financing for real estate transactions. The interest that is accrued on these REITs' assets is the primary source of revenue for the company.

To be recognized as a REIT, a business must demonstrate compliance with certain requirements outlined in the Internal Revenue Code (IRC). These conditions include distributing profits to shareholders regularly and focusing largely on the ownership of income-producing real estate over the long term. 3 To be eligible for status as a REIT, a corporation must, in particular, be able to demonstrate that it satisfies the following requirements:

- Invest at least 75% of total assets in either cash, real estate, or United States Treasuries.
- Real estate-related activities must provide at least 75% of the total gross revenue, either via rental income, interest on mortgages used to fund real property purchases, or sales of real estate.
- At least ninety percent of the annual taxable revenue must be distributed to shareholders in the form of dividends.
- You must be a legal entity that may be taxed as a company.
- Have a board of directors or trustees that are responsible for its management.
- After its first year of operation, have a minimum of one hundred investors in the company.
- Have no more than five persons own more than 50 percent of its shares at any one time.

1.6 REITs: A Guide to Investing in Them

You may purchase shares in publicly listed REITs, as well as REIT mutual funds and REIT exchange-traded funds (ETFs), via a broker. This is also the way to invest in REIT exchange-traded funds. You may purchase shares of a non-traded real estate investment trust (REIT) through a broker or financial adviser who takes part in the offering of the non-traded REIT. Additionally, real estate investment trusts are already being included into an expanding number of defined-benefit and defined-contribution investment plans. According to the research company NAREIT, which is located in Washington, D.C., there are around 145 million individuals in the United States who hold REITs either directly or indirectly via their retirement savings and other investment funds.

How does a REIT generate profits for its investors?

1.6.1 Income

Revenue is often earned through equity investments via sources such as rental payments from tenants, and this income is typically generated regularly. These could include the following:

- People who are renting a dwelling place for themselves.
- Commercial tenants who pay rent for their premises.
- Companies and organizations that rent out office space.

Income may be generated from debt investments via the receipt of loan interest payments, which are usually often made by a regular and established schedule of amortization.

1.6.2   Appreciation

If a REIT has direct ownership of a property, also known as equity ownership, then any gains in the value of the property, also known as appreciation, may affect the value of the REIT itself. As a result, the value of an individual share of a real estate investment trust (REIT) may increase in value if the properties that the REIT owns increase in value. On the other hand, the value of an individual share may decrease if the buildings lose value.

1.6.3   How can investors in REITs get profits on their investments?

REIT investors are eligible for the same sorts of returns that may be earned by real estate investment trusts (REITs), including income and appreciation of their investments. REIT investors usually obtain returns on their investments via dividend payments, which reflect the income produced by individual real estate holdings. This kind of investment is known as an income-generating investment. The REIT would normally make dividend payments to its investors consistently, with the amount of the payout being directly proportional to the investor's ownership stake in the overall fund.

In the meanwhile, for an investor to enjoy profits based on appreciation of their investment, the individual will often need to sell their REIT shares. In contrast to income, which may be paid out every month to an investor, appreciation is often achieved in a single, lump-sum payout upon the selling of shares. However, when a REIT sells an underlying property, capital gain dividends may be issued to investors even if those investors have not sold their shares in the

REIT. This is because investors are not required to sell their shares to receive the dividends. An investor is considered to have made a capital gain for any appreciation on an equity investment (REITs included) that was achieved in this manner, regardless of the kind of investment.

One of the primary reasons why many investors are drawn to REITs is the possibility that these investments can provide returns in the form of both capital appreciation and income. In addition, the two forms of returns can develop in tandem. Unlike many other sorts of investments, real estate is a hard asset, which means that there is a natural limit to the amount of it that can be produced. This gives real estate an inherent worth. The fundamental worth of a property can rise in tandem with an increase in its prospective rental revenue if there is an uptick in the demand for real estate. This is one of the primary reasons why real estate has been one of the best-performing asset classes throughout history.

1.7   Kinds of Investment

Based on the financial architecture of their underlying properties, there are three primary methods to classify real estate investment trusts (REITs):

- Debt
- Equity
- Combination of both

Both debt and equity investments come with their unique profit opportunities, and each kind of investment has its own set of repercussions for the possible return profile of an investor. This might include the frequency with which an investment will get returns as well as the process through which an investor will ultimately realize rewards.

1.7.1 Equity

An equity REIT is a kind of real estate investment trust that takes part in the direct ownership (and often the management and growth) of the real estate assets that it owns. These real estate assets may include commercial real estate as well as housing that is available for purchase. Many times, equity REIT managers may establish their investment strategy based on the amount of physical labor and financial commitment that they estimate is required to bring investment assets up to their maximum potential value and income-generating ability.

There are many types of real estate investment trusts (REITs) that fall under the more general category of equity REITs. These REITs are focused on certain equity strategies. For instance, an opportunistic equity REIT prioritizes properties that will need to have value added to them in the form of repairs or development before they can achieve their full potential in terms of both value and rental revenue. Other equity REITs may only buy already occupied income-producing properties that have been stabilized. These kinds of buildings demand far less direct labor and financial investment over the long run. Rental income from equity investments may frequently be large, with especially astute investments in rapidly developing regions offering the highest potential cash flow. This is because fast-growing locations have a greater demand for housing. Start your real estate investment portfolio with as little as ten dollars.

When it comes to real estate investments, the amount of labor that must be put in to make a property lucrative is often inversely proportional to both the return potential and the risk. As a result of the fact that equity real estate investments perform exceptionally well over extended investment horizons, it is common practice to include them as a natural component of an investment strategy that is designed to facilitate individual retirement or to construct a stable basis for an investor's financial situation.

Equity REITs provide several advantages, including a high potential for long-term development, including bigger relative returns and opportunistic methods, and no predefined limit on prospective return amounts.

- The possibility of generating money in the form of rental payments from tenants leasing properties controlled by the REIT.
- Equity Real Estate Investment Trusts Have a Few Drawbacks to Consider
- Equity investments may be subject to higher recurring expenditures due to the demands of property administration and/or renovations.
- The possibility for greater returns comes with a correspondingly increased level of risk.
- There are fewer protections available in comparison to investing in debt.

1.7.2   Debt

While some real estate investment trusts (REITs) put all of their money into stocks, others put all of their money into bonds. The value of debt in comparison to the value of equity is often contingent on the status of the economy and, more particularly, the trend in interest rates.

- Debt (or mortgage) investments are loans granted to equity owners in return for recurring repayments of principle with interest. This contrasts with equity real estate investments, which involve property ownership.
- Unlike equity investments, debt investments often include set conditions that describe the quantities of payment and the schedule of those payments from the borrower to the lender. This contrasts with equity investments, which do not have these stipulations. Amortization plans can include hard stops dates, or they might just be left open-ended.
- The return potential on debt investments is often not as great as the return potential on equity investments; and yet, the relative constancy of debt and the potential cash flow it might provide offer advantages that are their own.

Benefits of Investing in Debt REITs

- A great number of mortgage or debt REITs, which are collectively referred to as merit's, are seen as having significant yield potential. As was just said, these payments are often counted as income and distributed to investors in the form of dividends.
- Because of the positions their assets hold within the capital stack, debt REITs have the potential to have a low level of overall risk. If a security is declared in default, the capital stack is the system that determines the order in which investors are repaid for their investments. Mortgage REIT properties benefit from

advantageous capital stack placement, which makes them appealing to investors with a reduced risk tolerance.

Disadvantages of Debt REITs

- There is no limitless room for expansion.
- Interest rates have a significant impact on the amount of profit that may be made from loans.

1.7.3   Hybrid REITs

Hybrid real estate investment trusts (REITs) put their money into a combination of equity and debt real estate holdings, as its name suggests.

- A Look at the Benefits of Hybrid Real Estate Investment Trusts
- Hybrid real estate investment trusts can support both long-term development via the appreciation of equity investments and income production through debt investments and rental revenue.
- A hybrid real estate investment trust can explore any real estate investment that looks to have potential by using a mixed strategy that takes use of both loan and equity investments.
- A hybrid real estate investment trust is better equipped to resist the influence of external market forces as a result of the fact that its portfolio of properties includes a variety of investment formats.

Disadvantages of Hybrid REITs

A hybrid real estate investment trust (REIT) that does not place a significant emphasis on either equity or debt may not be able to offer extraordinary results in terms of either income or long-term appreciation.

1.8   Roles in a REIT

The following are examples of significant jobs that are often included in a REIT structure:

1.8.1   Trustee

The trust deed contains provisions that outline the obligations of the trustee. On behalf of the unit holders, the trustee is in charge of safeguarding the real estate investment trust's assets. Other responsibilities can include ensuring that all relevant laws are followed and safeguarding specific rights held by unit holders. For delivering this function, the trustee receives payment in the form of a fee.

The REIT manager is responsible for determining the REIT's overall strategic direction and putting that direction into action by the REIT's declared investment plan. For instance, it is responsible for the purchase and sale of properties owned by the REIT. In a real estate investment trust (REIT) model that is managed externally, the REIT manager receives payment for their services in the form of a management fee that comprises both a base fee and a performance fee. It may also levy other fees, such as those associated with acquisitions and sales.

The management of a real estate investment trust (REIT) is often entrusted to a separate entity known as a property manager. It is the role of the property manager to rent out the property to obtain the optimal tenancy mix and rental revenue, to organize and operate marketing events and programs to attract shoppers and renters, and to maintain the property in good repair. As a thank-you for their services, the real estate investment trust (REIT) pays the property manager a property management fee out of its assets.

1.8.2   REIT sponsor

There are several instances in which a sponsor is involved in the acquisition of properties for the first portfolio of a real estate investment trust (REIT). This sponsor may also continue to provide the REIT with a pipeline of assets. In most cases, the sponsor also has ownership in the REIT management as well as the REIT itself.

1.8.3   Rights as a unit holder in a REIT

In general, they are restricted to the power to do the following: Require the REIT management or trustee to run the REIT in compliance with the conditions of the trust deed. Unit holders need to call for a general meeting to remove a REIT management. During this meeting, they will vote on a motion to remove the REIT manager. At least fifty unit holders are required to submit a written request for a general meeting to the REIT management or trustee. Alternatively, the number of unit holders must equal or exceed 10% of the total number of units that have been issued by the REIT. After that, the motion to fire the REIT management must be approved by a simple majority of the unit holders who are present and voting at the general meeting, and there may be no disenfranchised unit holders.

1.9   REIT Fraud

When it comes to buying real estate investment trusts (REITs), the Securities and Exchange Commission (SEC) advises investors to be aware of anybody who attempts to sell them REITs that aren't registered with the SEC. It is recommended that "Using the EDGAR system provided by the SEC, it is possible to validate the registration of real estate investment trusts (REITs), whether they are publicly traded or not. You may also utilize EDGAR to study the annual and quarterly reports of a REIT, in addition to any offering prospectus that may be available." Checking up on the broker or financial adviser that suggests the REIT is something else that should be done. You may check to see whether an investing professional is licensed and registered by using the SEC's free search tool, which is located on their website.

REITs are required to distribute at least 90% of their taxable income, in the form of dividends, to their shareholders by the rules and regulations established by the IRS. As a direct consequence of this, most forms of corporate income tax do not apply to REIT businesses. REIT shareholders that receive dividends are subject to the same taxation as shareholders of companies that pay conventional dividends.

1.10   Advantages and Disadvantages of REITs

Advantages:

The following are some of the advantages of REITs:

- **Diversification**. When you invest in a pool of properties via a REIT, the risk that would have been incurred by investing in a single piece of real estate is spread out among all of those assets.

- **Affordability**. If you are an individual investor, you may not be able to afford a direct investment into a huge asset such as office buildings or retail malls. However, you may be able to afford an indirect investment. When you participate in a real estate investment trust (REIT), you have the opportunity to invest in enormous properties in manageable portions.
- **Liquidity**. Liquidity is the ability to acquire and sell units in a REIT more quickly and easily than buying and selling individual properties. You may trade individual units in a real estate investment trust (REIT) during a trading day if the REIT is listed on a stock market.
- **Tax benefits.** REITs that release at least 90% of their taxable revenue each year are afforded tax transparency by IRAS, which results in several financial advantages (subject to certain conditions). Individual shareholders who are beneficiaries of these dividends are likewise afforded the benefit of a tax-free status.
- **Transparency and flexibility**. You have access to information on REIT pricing and may trade REITs at any time throughout the trading day, providing you with both transparency and flexibility.

Disadvantages
Some of the risks associated with investing in REITs include:

Market risk

REITs are traded on the stock exchange and the prices are subject to demand and supply conditions.

The prices generally reflect investors' confidence in the economy, the property market and its returns, the REIT management, interest rates, and many other factors.

Income risk

Distributions are not guaranteed and are subject to fluctuations in the REIT's income. For example, a REIT's rental income may be affected if tenancy agreements could be renewed at a lower rental rate than before or the occupancy rate could fall.

Look out for whether the REIT has procured payment upfront or has contractual lock-ins of rental rates and other clauses in tenancy agreements.

If the underlying properties are financed by debts, there is a refinancing risk when cost of debt varies. A higher cost of debt may

also reduce the income
distributions to unit holders.

**Concentration
risk**

If a substantial portion of the
REIT's value is from one or a few
properties or a few tenants, you
face a greater risk of loss should
something happen to one of them.

Liquidity risk

A REIT may find it difficult to find
buyers and sellers for its
properties.
It may be difficult for REITs to
vary their investment portfolio or
sell its assets on short notice under
adverse economic conditions or
exceptional circumstances.

Leverage risk

Where a REIT uses debt to finance
the acquisition of its properties,
there is leverage risk.
If the REIT is wound up, its assets
will be used to pay off creditors
first. Any remaining value will
then be distributed to unit
holders.

Michael Allard

| **Refinancing risk** | As REITs distribute a large amount of their income to unit holders, they may not have the ability to build up cash reserves to repay loans as they fall due. |

Refinancing risk

As REITs distribute a large amount of their income to unit holders, they may not have the ability to build up cash reserves to repay loans as they fall due.

To refinance, they may need to borrow more (through bank borrowings or bond issuances) or undertake equity fund raising activities such as rights issues or private placements.

The refinancing cost could also be higher when loans are due for renewal.

Another risk is that the REIT is unable to secure refinancing and has to sell off some properties if they are mortgaged under the loan.

These risks could affect the unit price and income distribution of a REIT.

Land lease expiry risk

Where a REIT holds leasehold properties, the remaining term of the land leases will decrease over time, and the properties will have to be returned to the lessors upon the expiry of the land leases. The value of the REIT may be affected by the decreasing term or the expiry of the land leases, and this may result in a decline in the price of the units.

Other risks

While some REITS can offer diversity based on the type of properties or region you want to invest in, such diversification could carry other risks such as sector and country regulation risk.

Chapter 2

Why Invest in REITs?

The United States Congress came up with the idea of real estate investment trusts (REITs) so that ordinary people might own real estate. The framework made the playing field more accessible to everyone, when before it was only open to those with a significant amount of wealth. Investing in real estate investment trusts (REITs) may now be accomplished with a few mouse clicks by almost anybody who has access to the internet, a brokerage account, and some extra cash. In general, investing in REITs has shown to be profitable throughout their history. The following is a more in-depth examination of the reasons why investors need to think about include REITs in their portfolios.

2.1   Fundrise and eREITs

Fundrise is the first real estate investment platform that has created a simple and low-cost way for anyone to invest in private market real estate, for as little as $10, and access its historically consistent returns in the form of dividends and appreciation. Fundrise is also the first real estate investment platform that has created a way for anyone to invest in public market real estate for as little as $10. With the introduction of Fundrise eREITs, the first-ever entirely online real estate investment trusts, the company Fundrise has reimagined REITs for the internet era. These eREITs feature diverse portfolios. As a consequence of this, Fundrise eREITs provide investors with distinctive benefits that were previously unavailable to the majority of investors:

- Fundrise eREITs, which are classified as investments in the private market, provide meaningful diversification to the vast majority of investors. This is because their performance is significantly less correlated to the volatility of investments in the public market than the performance of their public counterparts.
- Fundrise eREITs have low costs and low fees since they are distributed directly to investors via Fundrise's web platform, which is a direct distribution channel. This strategy gets rid of the intermediaries that many conventional investing strategies still depend on, which gets rid of the layers of charges that eventually reduce the return potential of an investment.
- Investing in Fundrise eREITs, as opposed to other private market investments, may provide investors with restricted access to liquidity via the use of our various redemption plans.*
- eREITs are distinct funds that do not fit into any of the usual categories for REITs, even though their operations are most comparable to those of public non-traded REITs. They are subject to oversight by the SEC, which mandates that they comply with stringent reporting standards, such as conducting yearly audits and providing consistent financial updates.
- Both accredited and non-accredited investors are welcome to participate in Fundrise's offerings.

Here you will discover information that will assist you in setting your very own investing account at Fundrise, which will be stocked with a varied selection of real estate investments.

2.2   Why are REITs popular?

In addition to providing broad access to an asset class that would generally be out of reach for the majority of individual investors, many REITs may provide this access at a lower investment minimum and with a lower degree of risk than traditional ways of investing. And perhaps most critically, they simplify the process of gaining access to real estate.

How are these advantages obtained by real estate investment trusts? To begin, they provide average investors with exposure to real estate, including commercial real estate as well as other types of real estate, without the significant levels of risk that are associated with direct ownership. One of the numerous resources that are required up front and on an ongoing basis from an investor is a sizable initial quantity of money for the down payment. Direct ownership demands these resources. In addition, a significant amount of knowledge and experience in real estate, sound financial judgment, and continual property management are required to guarantee that a direct investment in real estate operates efficiently and generates a good net return.

In addition to these challenges, direct ownership sometimes necessitates the investment of a significant sum of money by the owner in a single asset throughout the term of that investor's ownership. The number of investments that the majority of investors can make is naturally restricted because this restricts the amount of cash that is available to the investor. As a result, the investors' risks are concentrated in just one or a few assets. On the other hand, real estate investment trusts (REITs) often own a portfolio of assets. This allows shareholders to diversify their holdings across numerous real estate properties. This raises the portfolio's overall risk-adjusted return potential while also lowering the risk of each investment in the portfolio.

In a similar vein, real estate investment trusts (REITs) provide investors with the ability to invest in a diverse range of real estate, which is something that they would not be able to do otherwise. A piece of real estate might be classified as belonging to any one of the several categories that make up the real estate market, such as residential or commercial construction, healthcare facilities, or even industrial projects. A real estate investment trust (REIT) may provide diversity in terms of both quantity and category.

Last but not least, in contrast to the majority of direct ownership opportunities, purchasing shares in a REIT may be accomplished with only a few clicks of the mouse. Before taking any steps toward real investing, it is essential for a potential investor to, as was said before, do all of the proper research and due diligence, educate oneself, and gain the skill to evaluate investment options.

2.3   Why REITs make a good investment

REITs provide investors with several advantages, which enables them to be an excellent addition to any investment portfolio. These characteristics include competitive long-term performance, appealing income, liquidity, transparency, and diversity.

2.3.1 Competitive long-term performance

When compared to equities, REITs have traditionally generated superior returns, particularly throughout extended periods. For instance, real estate investment trusts (REITs), as assessed by the FTSE NAREIT Composite Index, have generated a compound annual average total return of 11.4% over the last 45 years. This total return accounts for stock price increase as well as dividend income. That is just a somewhat lower rate of return than the S&P 500's average annual return of 11.5% throughout that period.

There have been times when the performance of REITs has been superior to that of equities. For instance, in the most recent three, five, ten, fifteen, twenty, twenty-five, thirty, thirty-five, and forty-year periods, they have outperformed small-cap equities as assessed by the Russell 2000 Index. The last twelve months have been the only time that small-cap stocks have outperformed REITs. In the meanwhile, real estate investment trusts (REITs) have outperformed large-cap equities (as measured by the Russell 1000 Index) throughout the last 20, 25, and 30 years. Last but not least, over the last four decades, they have consistently outperformed bonds across each historical phase.

2.3.2 Attractive source of revenue

One of the reasons why real estate investment trusts have been able to create strong overall returns over the long term is because the majority of REITs pay attractive dividends. For instance, the average yield on a REIT was over 3% as of the middle of 2021, which was more than twice the dividend yield on companies included in the S&P 500. This income, which accounts for the majority of a REIT's overall return throughout its entire existence, accrues steadily over time.

To stay in compliance with the requirements set out by the IRS, REITs are required to distribute ninety percent of their taxable revenue in the form of dividends. However, the majority of REITs distribute more than ninety percent of their taxable income. This is because their cash flows, as measured by funds from operations (FFO), are frequently significantly higher than their net income. This is because REITs tend to record significant amounts of depreciation each year.

Numerous REITs have impressive histories of successfully raising their dividend payments on an ongoing basis. For instance, Federal Realty Investment Trust increased its yearly dividend payment by 53 percent in 2021, making it the REIT industry's longest streak of consecutive dividend hikes. A great number of other REITs have maintained extended streaks in which they have raised their dividends at least once year.

2.3.3 Liquidity

An illiquid investment cannot be easily converted into cash, and real estate is considered to fall into this category. Take, as an example, the scenario in which the owner of a single-family rental (SFR) property found themselves in need of liquidating their investment to fund a significant expense. In such event, they would have no choice except to advertise the home, keep their fingers crossed that they get an offer that they can accept, and hope that the closing process goes well. Depending on the state of the market, it may be many months before they can turn the property into cash. They would most likely also be responsible for paying the commission to the real estate agent, in addition to the other expenditures associated with the closing.

On the other side, if an investor in a REIT needed money, they could log in to their online brokerage account whenever the market was open and sell their REIT shares. This would allow them to get the money they needed. Since the majority of brokers do not charge commissions, a REIT investor would not have to pay any costs to sell the investment.

2.3.4   Transparency

There is a generally lax level of monitoring for many private real estate ventures. Real estate sponsors often find themselves in a position where they must make judgments that aren't necessarily in the best interest of their investors. On the other hand, REITs are very open and honest. REITs' performance is monitored by a variety of parties, including independent directors, analysts, auditors, and members of the financial media. They are obligated to provide the SEC with reports on their financial outcomes as well. Investors in REITs are afforded a certain degree of protection by this regulation, making it more difficult for management teams to use the investors for their benefit.

2.3.5   Diversification

Investors can diversify their portfolios throughout the commercial real estate sector thanks to the availability of

REITs, which helps lessen the connection between their portfolios and the stock and bond markets. This diversity helps reduce the overall risk profile of an investor without having a detrimental influence on the rewards they get.

For instance, a classically balanced portfolio consisting of sixty percent equities and forty percent bonds has, on average, generated a return of little more than seven and a half percent over the last twenty years, with a Sharp Ratio of twenty-seven and a standard deviation of ten. A higher number for the Sharp Ratio indicates that an investment has a more desirable risk-adjusted return since it assesses risk in comparison to a risk-free investment such as a bond issued by the United States Treasury. The standard deviation, on the other hand, is a statistical measurement of volatility; a greater figure indicates an investment that is more susceptible to price swings. For comparison, a more aggressive method, consisting of 80% equities and 20% bonds, has historically yielded returns of around 8.3%, despite having a Sharp Ratio of 0.17 and a standard deviation that is higher than 13.

The inclusion of REITs in a portfolio results in stable returns while simultaneously lowering the associated risk. Take, for instance:

- A portfolio that is composed of 55% stocks, 35% bonds, and 10% REITs has, on average, generated a yearly return of around 8.3%, but it has only a Sharp Ratio of 0.34 and a standard deviation of about 10.5.
- Historically, a portfolio that is composed of 40% stocks, 40% bonds, and 40% real estate investment trusts has had an annualized return of little more than 8.4%, with

a Sharp Ratio of 0.46 and a standard deviation of less than 10.
- An investment portfolio consisting of 33.3% each in equities, bonds, and REITs has generated an average annual rate of return that is close to 9%, along with a Sharpe Ratio of 0.49 and a standard deviation of roughly 11.5.

Therefore, including real estate investment trusts in a portfolio should make it possible for the portfolio to generate superior risk-adjusted returns since REITs should help level out volatility.

Chapter 3

REITs and Social Impact

In what ways are REITs contributing to the development of more sustainable communities? The term "social" refers to the procedures, rules, practices, and impacts that an organization has with respect to the individuals, both internal and external, with whom it interacts. As owners and operators of the physical environments in which people work, reside, and build community, the real estate investment trust (REIT) industry is well-positioned to create a lasting social impact by directly addressing social considerations that are most relevant to their employees, tenants, and neighborhoods. This will allow the REIT industry to make a positive contribution to society. Training for employees on topics like as health and safety, diversity and inclusion, and creative employee wellness programs and strategic community collaborations are examples of some of the social initiatives being implemented throughout the sector.

Although real estate investment trusts (REITs) have been investing in social impact programs for quite some time, the sector as a whole shown a significant increase in the rates of reporting and disclosure in 2019 about important social policies, performance, and effect. In 2019, every single one of the NAREIT members who were polled said that they had a stance on social problems.

The following are some of the most often cited areas of concentration:

- Tenant engagement
- Community development
- Employee development programs
- Projects focusing on diversity, equality, and inclusion
- Programs focusing on health, safety, and overall wellbeing

REITs have reported greater staff retention, reputational benefits, and rising internal support to continue investing in and developing programs to strengthen their social impact. This is in addition to increased reporting and participation with social efforts. The coordinated effort that the REIT industry is making to increase the amount of formalized environmental, social, and governance (ESG) reporting demonstrates an evolving recognition and understanding of how the numerous initiatives that REITs have long undertaken to build thriving communities drive good business and fit within larger strategic efforts and support global sustainability goals. REITs are increasingly adopting social objectives and targets that are associated with UN Sustainable Development Goals that are important to the real estate business. This is similar to the situation with environmental sustainability.

3.1 REITs Create Value through Engagement

REITs have made stakeholder engagement a priority because they recognize its importance as a vehicle for recognizing, comprehending, and reacting to environmental, social, and governance-related opportunities and challenges. REITs are dedicated to being good neighbors and active participants in the communities in which they do business by implementing formal employee engagement initiatives, tenant engagement programs, and community engagement programs. One trend that has recently emerged among REITs is a greater emphasis on entering into meaningful partnerships that contribute to the overall goal of each organization while also satisfying the functional requirements of tenants and people of the community, as well as to enhance the performance of the company. Some have formed partnerships with suppliers and service providers in order to offer amenities and educational opportunities that contribute to tenant happiness and retention, as well as increase both businesses' environmental sustainability.

Others are collaborating with local partners to find solutions to the problems of both affordable housing and homelessness. Still others have formed alliances with pre-existing educational charities in order to provide financial assistance to community-based educational projects. Among these are initiatives that aim to assist members of underserved communities in acquiring the skills necessary to compete for jobs in today's labor market. REITs have used employee engagement as a tool to drive important social projects, as well as to better assure employee health, well-being, and pleasure with their place of employment.

96% of responding REITs offer their employees the opportunity to participate in company-sponsored community engagement and volunteer activities in their local communities, according to the 2019 NAREIT Member Survey. These activities can range from community blood drives and tutoring programs to individual initiatives to educate tenants on waste and water management.

3.2   How REITs become popular

In addition to providing broad access to an asset class that would generally be out of reach for the majority of individual investors, many REITs may provide this access at a lower investment minimum and with a lower degree of risk than traditional ways of investing. This is because REITs are structured as companies rather than as individual real estate holdings. And probably most importantly, they make it easier to get access to real estate markets by streamlining the application process.

How exactly do real estate investment trusts manage to have access to these benefits? To begin, they give average investors exposure to real estate, including commercial real estate as well as other types of real estate, without the significant levels of risk that are associated with direct ownership of real estate. This includes both residential real estate and other types of real estate. A sizeable initial sum of money for the down payment is one of the many resources that are expected from an investment right away as well as on a continuing basis. The direct ownership of these resources is required. In addition, a substantial amount of expertise and experience in real estate, as well as solid financial judgment and ongoing property management, are necessary to ensure that a direct investment in real estate functions well and delivers a fair net return. These are the requirements.

In addition to these issues, direct ownership sometimes requires the investor to invest a large quantity of money in a single asset for the duration of that investor's ownership of the asset. This is in addition to the challenges listed above. Because doing so reduces the quantity of liquid assets that investor has access to, the majority of investors are unable to make as many investments as they would want to. As a consequence of this, the investors' risks are centered on a single or a small number of assets. On the other hand, real estate investment trusts, sometimes known as REITs, frequently have a collection of assets under their control. Shareholders are given the opportunity to diversify their interests across a variety of real estate properties as a result of this. This not only lowers the risk associated with each individual investment in the portfolio, but it also improves the total risk-adjusted return potential of the portfolio as a whole.

In the same manner, real estate investment trusts (REITs) provide investors the opportunity to invest in a wide variety of real estate, which is something that they would not be able to do otherwise. This is something that is not possible for investors to accomplish without REITs. A piece of real estate may be categorized as belonging to any one of the numerous categories that make up the real estate market, such as residential or commercial construction, healthcare facilities, or even industrial projects. This is because the real estate market is comprised of a variety of different types of transactions. The variety that may be provided by a real estate investment trust (REIT) might come in the form of both quantity and category.

Last but not least, in contrast to the vast majority of options for direct ownership, acquiring shares in a REIT may be achieved with no more than a few clicks of the mouse. This is a significant time savings opportunity. It is crucial for a prospective investor to, as was said before, perform all of the necessary research and due diligence, educate oneself, and obtain the ability to assess investment possibilities before taking any moves toward actual investing.

3.3   What Opportunities Exist Related to Supply Chain Management?

REITs are becoming more interested in the management and control of supplier chains, and as a result, an increasing number of companies are including ESG standards into their procurement procedures. The number of real estate investment trusts (REITs) who claim to have a screening policy or method that has been made publically available to review suppliers' compliance with human rights standards and social practices is growing.

REITs that are at the forefront of ESG-related supply chain management have penned, implemented, and integrated supplier codes of conduct into their procurement requirements. These REITs are also considered to be leaders in the field. In 2019, REITs that reported to GRESB said that 84 percent of them evaluated the sustainability standards for their external suppliers and/or service providers.

Administration of the supply chain because supply chains may stretch through numerous layers and across different continents, environmental, social, and governance (ESG) activities can be complicated. 58% of the top 100 REITs ranked by stock market valuation have disclosed on their supplier screening criteria, which is an increase from only 22% in the previous year. This was done in an attempt to enhance the global supply chain management and transparency.

The members of NAREIT are also working to integrate company diversity efforts into their supply chains. Seven percent of members reported having formal initiatives to track and promote the use of diverse suppliers, and twenty-five percent of members indicated that they plan to formally implement initiatives in the year 2020.

3.4   ESG Rank as a Priority

In recent years, there has been a growing demand for greater transparency across global supply chains. This demand has been fueled by the fact that natural disasters, public health crises such as COVID-19, and media spotlights on labor practices have all underscored the extensive need to effectively manage supply chain risks.

Even though the vendors throughout the value chain differ for each REIT sector and based on the operating and business model of each individual REIT, the industry as a whole has prioritized several overarching leading practices to help move the needle toward greater sustainability across its supply chains. The following are examples of high-impact initiatives:

- Continuous involvement of suppliers in discussions pertaining to environmental, social, and governance issues, with the goal of gaining a deeper understanding of suppliers' commitments, practices, and opportunities for change;

- The incorporation of ESG screening criteria into the procedures used to evaluate vendors;
- Providing or supporting training for suppliers on important ESG themes, such as the management and reporting of greenhouse gas emissions, labor and human rights policies, diversity and inclusion, and corporate responsibility programs; and,
- The incorporation of supply chain resilience key performance indicators into metrics of company success
- In what ways are health and safety being prioritized by businesses?

REITs have made it a priority to provide their workers with a place of employment that is both safe and healthy. The vast majority of REITs that were polled said that they now run health and safety programs, and an increasing number of REITs are beginning to make these programs available to tenants as well. The COVID-19 pandemic has shown both the efficacy of these programs and the possibilities to adjust present procedures to meet growing health and safety regulations for the benefit of staff, renters, and the communities in which they are located.

Implementation of effective governance procedures is a crucial component of building programs that are effective with regard to health and safety. REITs have demonstrated their commitment to exercising strong governance of health and safety issues by the fact that 96% of respondents to the NAREIT Member Survey reported that their organization identifies and/or assesses work-related employee health and safety risks.8 REITs also have a strong track record of addressing health and safety concerns. In addition, 64 percent of the top 100 real estate investment trusts (REITs) ranked by equity market capitalization reported information on existing occupational health and safety policies. This represents an increase of 30 percent compared to the data for 2018.

These programs vary from the basic fire and emergency training that one would anticipate in an office setting to the very specialized and intricate procedures that are required in industrial or medical environments. REITs are making efforts to ensure that these essential health and safety measures are in place not just for buildings that already exist, but also for structures that are being constructed from scratch and for large refurbishment projects. In 2019, 77% of NAREIT members reporting to GRESB claimed that their organization had an on-site health and safety coordinator throughout the building phase. This is in contrast to the average number of on-site health and safety coordinators reported by worldwide GRESB respondents, which was 38%.

3.5   How Companies Prioritizing Health & Safety?

Increasing public commitments to, and disclosure of, employee engagement, development, and health and well-being programs have been demonstrated by the top one hundred real estate investment trusts (REITs) ranked by equity market capitalization as part of a growing trend toward greater transparency in the real estate investment trust (REIT) industry.

A rising number of REITs report having programs to support the well-being and development of their employees, and they are elevating senior management supervision and responsibility for significant concerns related to employee well-being and development. For instance, 63 percent of the REITs that were examined provide flexible work programs, and 85 percent of them give possibilities for organized professional growth. Only 35 percent of the companies who were polled for the 2020 Employee Industry Trends Report said that they intend to expand their spending in employee health and well-being programs in the following year. The survey was conducted among a larger cross-section of corporate America.

3.6   Are REITs Building Diverse & Inclusive Environments

REITs are aware of the value that diverse teams provide to their business performance. This value comes in the form of the potential to capture a broader variety of viewpoints, ideas, and experience, as well as the capacity to appeal to various clients, customers, and other stakeholders. Diversity, on both the board and staff levels, helps real estate investment trusts (REITs) gain access to previously untapped markets, promote "diversity of thought" on leadership teams, and improve employee satisfaction. Diversity also helps REITs attract new employees.

According to the findings of a study conducted by GRESB in 2019, 91 percent of respondents working in the global real estate business ensure that their governing bodies and employee populations are diverse.

REITs have made strides in this area by implementing comprehensive diversity and inclusion efforts. These initiatives have improved female representation and pay fairness at the top levels of the business, while also providing anti-harassment training to all workers. According to a study conducted by McKinsey in 2018, businesses that had gender representation on their executive teams that was more diverse were 21% more likely to have above-average profitability in comparison to their peers that had less diversity. Similarly, businesses that had significantly more racial and ethnic diversity in their executive teams were more likely to outperform their peers.

Chapter 4

How to Invest in Different Types of Real Estate Investment Trusts

When putting up a portfolio consisting of stocks and bonds or other types of investments, real estate investment trusts (REITs) are an important factor to take into account. They provide a larger degree of diversity, the possibility of better total returns, and/or a reduction in overall risk. In a nutshell, the fact that they may offer dividend income in addition to gain in value is what makes them such an effective diversifier when compared to cash, bonds, and stocks. Whether it's the properties themselves or the mortgages on those properties, real estate investment trusts (REITs) hold and/or manage income-producing commercial real estate. This may include either the properties themselves or the mortgages on those properties.

You have the option of purchasing shares of the firms directly, doing so via an exchange-traded fund, or doing so through a mutual fund. There is a wide variety of REITs accessible to investors. In this section, we take a look at some of the most important types of REITS and the historical returns they have generated. You should have a better notion of when to purchase things and what to buy by the time you finish reading this article.

- Diversifying your portfolio via the use of REITs to invest in real estate may be beneficial, but not all REITs are made equal.

- Some REITs make direct investments in real estate and profit from rental revenue as well as management fees. Others choose to put their money into real estate debt, such as mortgages and products backed by mortgages.
- In addition, real estate investment trusts (REITs) have a propensity to concentrate on a particular segment of the property market, such as retail or shopping malls, hotels and resorts, healthcare and hospitals, etc.
- High dividend yields are one of the most significant advantages that real estate investment trusts (REITs) have to offer. REITs are mandated to distribute ninety percent of their taxable income to their owners.
- The vast majority of REIT payouts do not adhere to the criteria of "qualified dividends" provided by the IRS.

4.1 How to Invest in the 5 Different Types of Real Estate Investment Trusts

Historically speaking, real estate investment trusts have been one of the asset types that have performed the best among those that are accessible. The majority of investors consult the FTSE NAREIT Equity REIT Index to evaluate how the real estate market in the United States is doing. The index generated an average yearly return of 9.5% over the years 2010 and 2020. 2 More recently, the three-year average for REITs between November 2017 and November 2020 was 11. 25%, which was much higher than both the S&P 500 and the Russell 2000, which both clocked in at 9.07%. The Russell 2000's three-year average was 6.45%.

Real estate has traditionally provided a higher return for investors than fixed income, the conventional asset class that is used for the goal of generating income for investors. Both of these should be taken into consideration while constructing a portfolio.

4.1.1   Retail REITs

About a quarter of the investments made by REITs go into shopping malls and standalone retail establishments. This is the single largest investment of this kind ever made in the United States. If there is a shopping mall that you often visit, there is a good chance that it is owned by a REIT. When one is thinking about investing in retail real estate, the first step that should be taken is to investigate the retail business on its own. Is it in a financially sound position at the moment, and what are the projections for the next years?

It is essential to keep in mind that retail REITs generate revenue via the collection of rent from their tenants. If a lack of sales is causing merchants to have cash flow issues, they could likely be compelled to postpone or even fail on their monthly payments, which will ultimately lead to their being pushed into bankruptcy. At that time, it will be necessary to find a new renter, which is never a simple task. As a result, you must make investments in REITs that have anchor tenants that are as robust as possible. These include places like supermarkets and hardware and home improvement businesses.

After you have completed your analysis of the market, you should shift your attention to the REIT companies themselves. As with any other kind of investment, they must have healthy profitability, robust balance sheets, and as little debt as is humanly feasible, particularly the sort that is short-term. When the economy is in a state of decline, retail REITs that are sitting on considerable cash reserves will be provided with chances to purchase high-quality real estate at bargain rates. The most effectively managed businesses will capitalize on this opportunity. Having said that, there are longer-term issues for the retail REIT industry because more and more people are migrating their shopping to be done online rather than in traditional malls. The owners of space have continued to innovate to fill their space with offices and other tenants that are not retail oriented; yet, the subsector is now under pressure.

4.1.2   Residential REITs

These real estate investment trusts (REITs) own and manage rental apartment complexes with several families as well as mobile homes. Before making a hasty decision to invest in this kind of REIT, one has to give careful consideration to several issues beforehand. For instance, the regions of the nation with the lowest median property prices tend to have the best apartment markets compared to the rest of the country. Because of the high cost of single-family houses, a greater number of individuals are forced to rent in cities like New York and Los Angeles. This, in turn, allows landlords to demand higher prices each month for rent. As a direct consequence of this, the primary concentration of the largest residential REITs is often placed inside major metropolitan areas.

When looking at individual markets, investors should focus on factors that indicate population and employment growth. When there is a net influx of people into a city, it is often because employment opportunities have increased and the local economy is expanding. The combination of a declining vacancy rate and increasing rents is evidence that demand is becoming stronger. Residential real estate investment trusts should perform well so long as the unit supply in a given area stays limited and the demand for housing continues to increase. As is the case with all businesses, the most successful ones are often those who have the healthiest balance sheets and the greatest amount of accessible cash.

4.1.3   Health care real estate investment trusts

As the population of the United States continues to age and the expense of medical treatment continues to rise, it will be fascinating to keep an eye on the subsector known as healthcare REITs. The real estate of healthcare institutions, such as hospitals, medical centers, nursing homes, and retirement homes, is the focus of investment of healthcare REITs. The prosperity of this property is inextricably linked to the functioning of the healthcare system. The bulk of the people who run these establishments are supported financially by occupancy fees, reimbursements from Medicare and Medicaid, as well as private money. As long as the financing for healthcare remains uncertain, the future of healthcare REITs will be uncertain as well.

You should search for a healthcare REIT that has assets in a variety of property types as well as a diverse clientele when you are making your selection. Concentration is helpful up to a point, but it's also important to disperse your risk around. A rise in the demand for healthcare services (which is expected to occur with an older population) is generally beneficial for the real estate market in the healthcare sector. Therefore, in addition to looking for firms that have a diversified client base and portfolio of different types of properties, you should seek for businesses that have substantial expertise in the healthcare industry, solid balance sheets, and high levels of access to low-cost funding.

4.1.4 Office REITs

Office REITs are organizations that invest in office buildings. They collect rental money from occupants, who have often signed leases for extended periods. Anyone interested in investing in an office REIT should consider the following four questions.

- What is the current situation of the economy, and what is the percentage of unemployed people?
- How high are the percentages of available rooms?
- From an economic standpoint, how is the region in which the REIT invests faring?
- How much money does it have available for purchasing assets?

Look for real estate investment trusts that put their money into economically stable areas. When compared to, for instance, owning premium office space in Detroit, it is advantageous to possess a collection of ordinary buildings in Washington, District of Columbia.

4.1.5 Mortgage REITs

Mortgages account for around 10% of REIT assets, as opposed to the actual real estate holdings itself. Fannie Mae and Freddie Mac are government-sponsored firms that acquire mortgages on the secondary market. Although they are the most well-known investments, this does not always mean that they are the best. But the fact that this particular kind of REIT invests in mortgages rather than stock does not indicate that it is risk-free in any way. A rise in interest rates would result in a decline in the book values of mortgage REITs, which would lead to a reduction in stock prices. Additionally, a significant portion of mortgage REITs' capital comes through the sale of secured and unsecured debt issues. If interest rates go up, the cost of future borrowing will go up, which will result in a reduction in the value of a loan portfolio. In a climate characterized by historically low interest rates and the likelihood of those rates increasing shortly, the majority of mortgage REITs trade at a discount to their net asset value per share. The challenge is in selecting the appropriate one.

4.2 How to Evaluate Real Estate Investment Trusts

When evaluating any REIT, there are a few key points to keep in mind at all times. The following are some examples of them:

- REITs are truly total-return investments. They have substantial dividend yields in addition to having reasonable capital appreciation over the long term. 4 Look for businesses who have a solid track record in the past of successfully offering both services.

- In contrast to conventional real estate, many real estate investment trusts (REITs) are traded on stock markets. You get the benefits of diversification that real estate offers without being committed to a long-term investment. Liquidity matters.
- Depreciation tends to exaggerate the drop in property value caused by an investment. Therefore, when evaluating a REIT, rather than looking at its payout ratio (which is what dividend investors use), take a look at its funds from operations (FFOs). This is calculated by subtracting depreciation and any properties that were sold during the year from the net income. To calculate the dividend per share, just take the FFO per share and divide it by the dividend per share. The better the results, the bigger the yield should be.
- A difference may be seen when strong management is in place. Try to find businesses that have been in operation for a considerable amount of time or that at least have a management team that has a great deal of expertise.
- It's all about the quality. Only invest in real estate investment trusts that have excellent assets and renters.
- If you want to outsource the research and purchasing decisions, you can think about purchasing a mutual fund or an exchange-traded fund that invests in real estate investment trusts (REITs).

4.3 Effects of Real Estate Investment Trust

Similar to other types of investments, real estate investment trusts (REITs) come with both positives and negatives. One of the most significant advantages that real estate investment trusts (REITs) provide is high dividend yields. As a result of the fact that REITs are obligated to distribute 90% of their taxable income to their shareholders, REIT dividends are often substantially greater than the dividends paid by the average company on the S&P 500. 5

Diversification of the portfolio is still another advantage. The capacity to acquire a piece of commercial real estate to produce passive income is not available to a large number of individuals; nevertheless, real estate investment trusts (REITs) provide the general public with the opportunity to do so. In addition, the process of purchasing and selling real estate may take a significant amount of time, which might impede cash flow. On the other hand, REITs are highly liquid investments, and the majority of them can be purchased or sold with the simple click of a button.

Investors should be aware of the possible tax burden that might be created by REITs since this is the most significant disadvantage associated with REITs. Other disadvantages include: The majority of dividends paid by REITs do not satisfy the requirements set out by the IRS to be considered "qualified dividends." As a result, the above-average dividends paid by REITs are subject to a higher tax rate than the majority of other distributions. Although real estate investment trusts (REITs) are eligible for the pass-through deduction of 20% of qualified business income, the vast majority of investors will be required to pay a significant amount of taxes on REIT dividends if they hold REITs in a conventional brokerage account.

Another possible problem with real estate investment trusts is that they are sensitive to changes in interest rates. When the Federal Reserve raises interest rates to curb expenditure, real estate investment trust (REIT) values often decrease as a result. In addition, there are a variety of property-specific risks that are associated with the various kinds of REITs. Hotel real estate investment trusts, for instance, often perform very badly when the economy is in a downward spiral.

Pros

- Dividends with a high yield
- Portfolio diversification
- Highly liquid

Cons

- Dividends are subject to the same taxation as regular income.
- Vulnerability to changes in interest rates
- Dangers connected to certain aspects of the property

4.4 REIT FAQs

4.4.1 Are REITs Good Investments?

Strong dividends and sustained increase of value over the long run may make investments in real estate investment trusts (REITs) an appealing alternative to standard stock and bond investments as a means of diversifying one's portfolio.

4.4.2 What REITs Should I Invest In?

Depending on the trajectory of the economy, different kinds of REIT are exposed to varying degrees of risk and potential reward. The use of an exchange-traded fund (ETF) to invest in real estate investment trusts (REITs) is a terrific method for shareholders to participate in this industry without having to individually deal with the complexity of the industry.

4.4.3   How Do You Make Money on a REIT?

The Internal Revenue Service mandates that REITs distribute ninety percent of their taxable income to their shareholders. As a result, REIT dividends are often substantially greater than the dividends paid by the typical company on the S&P 500. The compounding of these high-yield dividends is one of the most effective methods to get passive income from real estate investment trusts (REITs).

4.4.4   Can You Lose Money on a REIT?

There is always the possibility of incurring a loss with every investment you make. When interest rates rise, investors often shift their wealth into bonds, which poses a unique risk of value erosion for publicly listed real estate investment trusts (REITs).

4.4.5   Are REITs Safe During a Recession?

During times of economic instability, it is not a wise decision to put money into certain kinds of real estate investment trusts (REITs), such as those that invest in hotel assets. Investing in other kinds of real estate, such as health care or retail, which have longer lease agreements and are thus far less cyclical, might be an excellent method to protect oneself financially in the event of an economic downturn.

4.5   Crux of the Matter

As early as 1960, the federal government opened the door for investors to participate in large-scale commercial real estate developments by making it feasible for them to do so. However, private investors have just begun to show interest in REITs in the last ten years. Low interest rates, which forced investors to look beyond bonds for income-producing investments, the advent of exchange-traded and mutual funds focusing on real estate, and, before the real estate meltdown of 2007-2008, an insatiable appetite on the part of Americans to own real estate and other tangible assets are some of the reasons for this trend. As was the case with almost every other kind of investment in 2008, REITs experienced significant losses. Despite this, they remain to be a valuable asset that should be included in every diversified investment portfolio.

Chapter 5

How to Get Started in Real Estate Investing

Increasingly, individuals choose to construct their portfolios by investing in real estate as a strategy to diversify their holdings. Historically speaking, investments in real estate have generated higher returns than certain other types of assets. In addition to this, it provides the potential investor with a variety of various choices. You may earn money in real estate by becoming a landlord and buying property for yourself, but you can also make money in real estate by purchasing shares in a Real Estate Investment Trust (REIT) or by lending money to other people who are investing in real estate.

5.1   Becoming a Landlord

Consider your options before making an investment. Before making any purchases, investors should have a plan for how they will eventually sell any property they own. Do you intend to buy, remodel, and then resell the property? Or, are you interested in leasing the property? When it comes to funding and taxes, each of these choices has various repercussions; thus, you will need to have a broad concept of which path you want to pursue from the beginning of the process and be prepared for any unexpected developments.

- For starters, you should have an accurate assessment of the breadth and depth of your skill set. Do you have the practical experience and industry expertise necessary to flip houses? You will need to have a fundamental understanding of the many types of property repairs as well as the expenses associated with common and less common types of repair work.

- Whether you want to sell the property or rent it out, you absolutely need to have a reserve money set up. This is a must. As a general guideline, an investor should have sufficient funds in reserve to pay the mortgage for a period of six months in the event that the property ends up being empty or is in a condition where it has to be rehabilitated before being sold. When you rent an apartment, you are also responsible for paying the renter's mortgage in a timely manner. In the event that your renter is late with their rent payment, having a reserve will assist you cover the cost of the payment.

5.1.1   Analyze profitability of available properties

Perform a cost-benefit analysis on each of the accessible properties. Make sure that the property you want to buy is going to turn a profit before you commit to buying it. Conduct an analysis of both the amount of rent or revenue you anticipate receiving and the running expenditures you now have. Take into account the community in which you want to purchase a home in order to ascertain whether or not houses in that area tend to hold onto their worth.

- Determine the price-to-rent ratio in the area where you wish to buy a home by doing the appropriate math. It is important to keep in mind that information on rent pricing is not always simple to get; thus, this value should only be regarded a rough estimate at best. Take the median yearly rent and divide it by the median price of a property. For illustration's sake, let's say the median price of a property is $180,000 and the typical yearly rent is around $12,000 ($1,000 per month). The ratio of purchase price to monthly rent is. The ratio should be as low as possible for the investment to be considered successful. It is not a smart idea to invest in a location that has a price to rent ratio that is more than 20.

- Determine the total gross rental income. Take the yearly rent and divide it by the total amount that was paid to acquire the property. This helps you select the home that has the most rental income while also having the lowest expenditure for the purchase. For instance, if you buy $100,000 for a home and you can rent it out for $12,000 a year, which breaks down to $1,000 per month, the gross rental yield for that home is 12. An acceptable rate of return for an investment is anything above 10%. [3] It may be necessary to make a substantial financial expenditure in order to make some homes habitable (such as installing a new roof or replacing the carpeting), but if the rental yield is high enough, a property that needs repair may still be considered a profitable investment.

- Calculate the capitalization rate. This will inform you the rate of return that you may expect from the revenue generated by the property. In most cases, the capitalization rate is determined by either the property's net revenue from the most recent year (if it was leased out) or the predicted rental income for the next year (if it is not currently being rented). Take the property's annual net revenue from operations and divide it by its acquisition price. The whole yearly revenue is subtracted from the operating expenses to arrive at the net operating income (running costs typically eat up roughly forty percent of the income). Imagine that you are interested in purchasing a property for the price of $500,000, and that you're anticipated monthly net operational income is $35,000. The rate of capitalization you would have would be 7%. This indicates that you would make a profit equal to seven percent of the value of the property. When comparing the profitability of several properties, use the capitalization rate as your benchmark.

- If the operating costs are not clear, or if you are just trying to get a very general idea as to whether or not the property is a good investment, take the purchase price and divide it by the total annual rent to find out how many years it will take to earn the money back. This can help you determine whether or not the property is a good investment. This can be helpful when comparing different properties; for example, if it will take one property five years to earn back the investment, while another property will take seven years, and the capital improvements are the same in both properties, then you should probably pursue the property that will earn your money back in a shorter amount of time.

- Determine the flow of funds. Determine whether the amount of rent you may charge will bring in enough money to pay the principle, interest, taxes, and insurance on the mortgage. Additionally, ensure that you have sufficient savings to handle unforeseen costs, such as those associated with repairs. If this does not happen, your cash flow will be negative, which puts you in danger of failing on your mortgage payment obligations.

5.1.2 Arrange Financing

To begin, it is quite probable that you will be required to make a sizable initial deposit in the form of a down payment. The majority of commercial loans call for initial deposits ranging from 25% to 35%. Consider taking out a personal loan, taking out a line of credit against the equity in your house, using your credit cards, or even cashing in a life insurance policy if you do not have a significant amount of cash on hand. Your interest rate will be determined by the amount of financial reserves you have in the bank and your credit score. Your credit score will be dependent on how well you have managed your finances in the past. Instead of dealing with a huge, national bank, you may want to think about working with a local bank. When it comes to the structure of a mortgage, local banks often give greater freedom.

You are not limited to making a down payment of 20% of the total. There is a possibility that you might qualify for FHA financing for owner-occupied properties with a down payment of as low as 3.5%. There is also the option of getting a hard money loan. These loans do not take into account your credit score in the decision-making process, so you may be able to acquire funding very quickly. However, the interest rate on these loans is normally very high and is very close to the usury rate. There is a possibility that hard money loans will work for flipping houses, but they are not suggested for long-term investments.

- If you want to know about all of your potential avenues of financial support, your best choice is to consult with an experienced broker. Conventional loans to investors are subject to a wide variety of limitations, in addition to predetermined limits. For example, you are only allowed to have one active FHA loan at any one time, and you are obliged by law to get commercial loans for properties that have five or more individual units. A broker can assist you in navigating your available alternatives and help you build a strategy to ensure that all of your finance requirements are met.
- Always tell your lenders the truth about the condition of the property. There are some categories of real estate that many financial institutions will not give money on, so if you want to prevent having your financing fall through in the future, you should supply the lender with photographs and information on any problems that the property has. You do not want the purchase to go through because the lender conducted an assessment and discovered that the property requires costly repairs or that there was severe damage to it.
- It is important to keep in mind that mortgage insurance, which shields the lender from loss in the event of default, does not apply to investment properties.

5.1.3   Shop for a property

Look around for a suitable home. To begin, take a look at the homes that are currently available on the multiple listing service (MLS). Websites like as Realtor.com, Trulia, and Zillow all provide access to the MLS listings on their own platforms. If you search the Multiple Listing Service (MLS), you will see all of the same listings that a real estate agent may locate for you. However, it is still recommended that you seek the assistance of a real estate agent. They could know more about the particular homes or the facilities offered by such places. In addition to this, they are likely to be aware of available homes that are not currently listed on the MLS.

When it comes to time, one of the most significant benefits of dealing with a realtor is that they will provide you an advantage over other people. They can sign you up to get rapid emails for properties that suit your criteria as soon as they go on the market or come back on the market, even before they appear on the websites of other real estate brokerages. In today's competitive real estate market, this is a very helpful service.

 Keep in mind that there are several topics on which a real estate agent is not permitted, by law, to remark. Your Real Estate Agent, for example, is unable to form an opinion on the "excellent" or "poor" qualities of a certain community. Make use of a tool such as RAIDS online to get an idea of the level of violence in the region and visit floodsmart.gov to learn more about the likelihood of flooding (requiring you to buy additional flood insurance for your property). Since real estate agents are often paid by the seller at the time of settlement, working with one may not always cost the buyer anything. However, purchasers could also be required to pay a commission to a buyer's agent as part of the transaction. This is something that may be discussed in a "For Sale by Owner" deal, and it may open up additional properties that are accessible for you to examine as possibilities.

5.1.4 Make your offer

Put up your proposal. Determine what a reasonable selling price would be for the property with the help of your real estate agent. In addition, be sure to include any inspection and finance stipulations, as well as any additional stipulations that your realtor or lawyer may recommend. Determine a date for the settlement that is convenient not just for you but also for the seller. There are some sellers who will agree to a sale at a cheaper price provided the settlement date that is being given is agreeable to them.

- Never buy a home without first having it examined to identify any potential issues that might cost you money in the future. In the event that the inspector discovers anything, you may be able to modify the terms of the agreement. You may be able to reduce your offer and make the necessary repairs on your own, ask the seller to do the repairs, or do a mix of all of these options.
- Be completely transparent about the examination. For instance, some lenders will not provide financing for a home if they are aware of a necessary repair that is of significant importance to them. It is in your best interest to settle any issues that may develop before to closing, and if those issues can't be resolved to your satisfaction, you should look into alternative houses.
- In most cases, you will want to make certain that the property satisfies all of the specified conditions, including the inspection. However, depending on the specifics of the situation, a buyer can decide to forego the inspections and go ahead and make the purchase nonetheless. For instance, given that some investors are ready to make repairs to a property and don't need

financing, they may purchase a home that wouldn't be able to pass inspection.

5.1.5 Find tenants

If you plan to rent out the property, you will need to find tenants for it. The ideal tenants would be ones who would pay their rent in full and on time, keep the property in good condition, and adhere to the rules that are outlined in the lease. If you plan to rent out the property, you will need to find tenants. When looking for renters, you should keep certain considerations in mind. Put up an ad looking for renters without targeting any one demographic in particular. Tenants are subjected to stringent screening.

- To get the word out about your property, advertise it via word of mouth, flyers, posters, print advertisements in local newspapers, and online ads on real estate websites. Rental listings may be posted for free on several websites, including Craigslist, Zillow, and others.
- Set your rent at a level that allows you to meet your running costs, make a profit that is appropriate for your business, and remain competitive with other rentals in the region. You are required to apply the same standards to everyone.
- Applicants should be given a list of the rental criteria that will be used to assess them in the application process.
- Require all potential candidates to fill out an application that not only provides their contact information, but also their income sources, prior addresses, and names of references. Also, make sure you have their consent before checking their credit or verifying their income.

Check with their employers to verify their claims of income after you have received authorization to do so. You are able to check someone's credit with any one of the three major credit reporting agencies as soon as you obtain their Social Security number and permission to do so. To verify references, get in touch with your former landlords.

5.1.6 Evaluate potential candidates

Applicants for rentals might be screened based on characteristics that exclude them from being considered. These may contain things like your credit score, your gross income, your rental history, and your criminal record. A past eviction may result in negative consequences, such as being denied for housing or owing money to a former landlord. Make sure to provide applicants a comprehensive list of the criteria you will be using to assess them. These criteria are up to you, as long as you don't discriminate against any groups that are legally protected or breach any laws at the state or federal level.

Get familiar with any federal, state, or municipal legislation that could prevent different groups of individuals from being discriminated against. The Civil Rights Act, for instance, makes it illegal to discriminate against people on the basis of their race. A person is guaranteed to be treated fairly under the Fair Housing Act regardless of their race, color, national origin, religion, sex, handicap, or whether or not they have children.

- You have the ability to insist on specific conditions, such as a bigger deposit or a co-signer, in the event that you choose to accept an application who has concerns.

However, if you decide to reject an application or accept them with additional restrictions, you will need to write them a letter detailing the unfavorable decision and the reasoning behind it.

- There are businesses out there that are able to provide expert screening services. Applicants will often cover the cost of this service on their own, taking you out of the equation for the investigation. After that, after you get the data, you may do more analysis and determine if any additional conditions are necessary.

5.2 Purchasing Shares in a Real Estate Investment Trust

Gain an understanding of what is meant by the term "real estate investment trust" (REIT). Real Estate Investment Trusts (REITs) are businesses that either own or manage commercial real estate. They make it possible for people to get financial benefit from real estate revenue without the need of purchasing commercial property.

5.2.1 Choose a type of REIT in which to invest

Make a decision about the kind of REIT in which you want to invest. There is a wide variety of fields in which real estate investment trusts (REITs) might be invested. REITs in each sector have their own unique methods for generating revenue from real estate investments. When selecting a kind of REIT, it is important to take into consideration the health of the broader economy as well as the performance of the industry in question.

- Shopping malls and standalone retailers are both included in the scope of retail REITs. They are able to turn a profit on the rent that they collect from their renters. Make a decision to invest in retail real estate investment trusts (REITs) when the retail business is thriving and sales are robust.

- Residential REITs are the owners of apartment complexes with several units. They also earn money off of the rent that they collect from their renters. The most lucrative environments for residential REITs are big metropolitan regions with high housing prices that require a significant portion of the population to rent rather than buy. This causes rent rates to rise, which in turn boosts the REIT's overall profitability. The profitability of a residential REIT is impacted not only by the rate of vacancy, the number of construction licenses granted, and the presence or absence of rent control in the region, but also by the pace of job growth in the area.

- Hospitals, nursing homes, medical centers, and retirement homes are all eligible investments for healthcare REITs. As a result of people living longer and having an increased need for these services, this industry is growing more lucrative. They generate revenue from the governmental healthcare system.

- Office REITs are landlords of office spaces. Long-term leases in the office buildings are the primary source of revenue for them. Before making a decision to invest in an office REIT, it is important to take into account both the current status of the economy and the unemployment rate. Consider the state of the economy in the region where the REIT is located as another factor in your analysis. Some urban areas are suffering from economic downturns, while others are showing signs of economic expansion.

- Mortgage REITs, as opposed to investing in actual property, make investments in mortgages and mortgage-backed securities.

5.2.2 Purchase shares in an REIT

Buy a stake in a real estate investment trust. Get in touch with a broker or a financial counselor in order to locate the REIT investment that best suits your needs. Purchasing positions in REITs may be accomplished via a wide range of distinct channels. Some of them are traded in the public market on stock exchanges. Others are privately traded or are not publicly traded at all. Buying shares in a real estate investment trust via a mutual fund or exchange-traded fund is still another possibility (ETF).

- The Securities and Exchange Commission (SEC) has granted registration to a great number of real estate investment trusts (REITs), and these REITs can be found listed on major stock markets including the New York Stock Exchange (NYSE).
- Public non-listed and private REITs are both required to be registered with the SEC; however, none of these types of REITs are traded on any stock market.
- If you don't want the hassle of picking a particular real estate investment trust (REIT) to invest in, you may acquire shares in a mutual fund or exchange traded fund that invests in REITs instead. Investing firms like as Vanguard, Fidelity, and JPMorgan Chase & Co. are good places to look for these types of products. The investing firm investigates the current situation of the

real estate market and constructs a portfolio that is optimized to provide the maximum possible return.

5.3   Lending Money to Other Real Estate Investors

Gain an understanding of the concept of lending money privately. Lending your own money to another investor or to a real estate fund that is managed by professionals is what is meant by the term "private money lending." If you have already been successful with some of your previous real estate investments and are looking for a method to reinvest some of the money that you have gained, this may be something that interests you. You, as a private money lender, provide as an alternative to traditional financial institutions like banks and other financial companies. Your debts are protected by the value of the real estate you own.

- Working with private money lenders is popular among investors because it enables them to get funds in a timely manner without being subject to the stringent rules that are enforced by banks. Additionally, there is a high degree of openness throughout the process.
- Private money lenders, also known as hard-money lenders, often demand higher interest rates than banks do and anticipate being repaid in a shorter amount of time, typically somewhere around 5 years. Unless the property is sold before the payment on the mortgage is due, they are designed for investors who more often trade than rent real estate. On the other hand, they often accept higher-risk loans than a bank would be willing to sanction, such as loans for houses that the owner intends to renovate and then sell or rent out.

5.3.1   Identify borrowers

Determine who the borrowers are. The real estate sector is seeing a considerable rise in the importance of private money lending as a source of finance. Investors are increasingly resorting to private money lenders in order to get funds in a timely manner. This is due to the increasingly stringent requirements imposed by banks and other lending organizations. Borrowers are drawn from a variety of sub-industries within the real estate market.

- People who are interested in flipping properties, for example, often check into these kinds of loans since the existing state of the property is irrelevant to the decision. In these circumstances, will need to be aware of both the existing worth of the property as well as the value that is anticipated after the property has been rehabilitated. Be careful to acquire an evaluation from a professional who is either a registered real estate agent or an appraiser.
- In order to finance their construction and development projects, builders, developers, and commercial investors often work with private money lenders. These sorts of risky investments are often avoided as much as possible by financial institutions like banks.

5.3.2   Mitigate danger

Examine the viability of possible loans to see whether or not they will result in a return on investment. When selecting whether or not to pursue an opportunity, it is important to take into consideration a number of different aspects. Loss of money may occur if the prospective benefits and dangers of an investment are not adequately weighed against one another.

- The majority of private money loans are somewhere from 60 to 70 percent of the property's current market value. The term "loan-to-value ratio" refers to the proportion of the loan amount to the current worth of the property on the market.
- You should investigate the borrower's equity in addition to determining whether or not they are creditworthy. Investigate whether or not they have sufficient equity in other properties to pay any sudden or unanticipated costs that may arise.
- If at all feasible, organize the loan in such a way that places you in the position of first lien holder. In the case that there is a breach of contract, this status designates you as the primary creditor who will be paid back. If you give a larger loan-to-value ratio, you will have a better chance of securing this lien priority.

5.3.3   Generate the proper loan documents

Produce the necessary documentation for the loan. The required documentation for a private money loan is comparable to that which is required for a conventional bank loan. The borrower is required to sign a promissory note, which is a legally binding document that states the borrower will return the debt. In addition, the borrower is required to provide additional security for the loan in the form of a mortgage on an existing property. In the case of residential real estate, private money loans often need the use of third-party appraisals, in-person property inspections, and geological reports, among other things.

Check with your lender to find out what regulations they have in place. It's also possible that you'll need the following papers.

- The agreement is described in detail in a letter of intent (LOI).
- The ultimate price of the acquisition as well as the conditions of the transaction are outlined in a buy and sell agreement.
- You are needed to get title insurance as well as a preliminary title report, which provides a history of the ownership of the property.
- A proof of funds is a bank statement or another document given by the borrower to demonstrate that they have the money available to repay the loan. This is done so that the lender may be certain that they will be repaid.
- If the borrower is unable to repay the loan, a personal guarantee from the borrower will specify which assets the borrower is able to sell to pay off the debt.
- Either a deed of trust or a mortgage may be used to make a property pledge in order to secure a loan.
- The borrower promises to reimburse you for any damages that result from environmental pollution of the property by signing an environmental indemnity agreement. This kind of arrangement is known as an environmental indemnity agreement.

Chapter 6

How to Get Started in the Real Estate Business

Investing in real estate is a tricky business that involves the constant movement of a significant amount of money. Adding real estate to your investment portfolio is one of the most common ways to increase the size of that portfolio. Investing your money wisely is possible with the guidance of this tutorial.

6.1   Understand the Market

Educate yourself on the topic of investing in real estate. It is important to do extensive study on the topic and get familiar with the workings of the market before attempting to make money investing in real estate. There are many different approaches to investing in real estate, and in order to choose the strategy that is most suitable for you, you will first need to consider your objectives and your financial situation.

- An interest in land" is the definition of real estate (and anything permanently attached to land). This indicates that the primary focus of buyers and sellers in the real estate market is the acquisition and disposal of land and structures. In the realm of real estate, "interest" may be broken down into two categories: ownership and leasehold. In the context of real estate, "leasehold interest" refers to the practice of transferring certain rights to a tenant in return for payment of rent, while "ownership interest" refers to the act of acquiring complete control and responsibility for land and buildings.

- Purchasing an ownership stake in a piece of real estate and then generating income from the rent that is collected from tenants is the most prevalent kind of real estate investment.

6.1.1 Identify your tolerance for risk

Determine how much of a risk you are willing to take. When it comes to real estate transactions, there are two primary markets to consider. Both private businesses and state entities participate in these marketplaces. All forms of investment include some degree of risk, although different markets have varying degrees of danger. The acquisition of an ownership interest in "real" property, as opposed to "personal" property, is required in order to invest in private real estate. The operation of that property would then be handled by either you or a property manager, and you would make money off of the rent that was paid by tenants. Because you, as the owner, are accountable for the property, this method of investing in real estate is one of the most straightforward methods.

Buying shares of a publicly listed real estate business is required in order to invest in public real estate. Investment trusts are often the structure that these kinds of businesses assume. You may purchase shares on the open market, and as the trust accumulates value and rent from the many properties it owns, you will be entitled to dividend payments. If you merely possess shares in the firm, then you do not have any responsibility for the property the company owns. Investing may also be done in a roundabout way like this.

6.1.2   Decide between equity and debt

Decide between equity and debt. Equity and debt are the driving forces behind the workings of both the public and private markets. As an investor, it is up to you to decide which of them you want to put your money into.

- Lending money to another person so that they might purchase an interest in a piece of real estate is what is meant by the term "investing in debt." When you have a mortgage, you will get money each month in the form of interest payments.
- Investing in equity is the same as investing in the ownership of the property, and the two terms are interchangeable. This indicates that you are willing to take on all of the obligations associated with the management of the land and the structures.

6.1.3   Choose the real estate sector you want to invest

Make a decision on the real estate submarket you want to invest in. The public equity, the public debt, the private equity, and the private debt markets are the four sectors.

- If you decide to participate in public equities, you should investigate the availability of investment trusts. If you decide to invest in public debt, you should look into mortgage securities. Mortgage securities are the debt equivalent of investment trusts, in which multiple mortgages are bundled together to form a single investment. If you choose to invest in public debt, you should investigate mortgage securities.

- If you decide to go the route of private equity, then you will most likely become a landlord and make investments in either residential or commercial real estate. If you decide to choose the private debt route, then your investments will be in private mortgages.

6.1.4   Learn about real estate trading

Gain an understanding of the real estate transaction process. This is a subset of private equity investment that takes the form of flipping, another name for the practice. The objective is to first buy a piece of real estate and then resale it at a greater price than what you paid for it. In order to reduce their total expenses of ownership as much as possible, these investors work hard to swiftly sale the properties they hold.

The majority of people who flip houses do not make any modifications to the homes they purchase since doing so may be both costly and time consuming. Instead, they put their money on the market turning in their favor so that they may resell the home without making any changes and make a profit. During a real estate transaction with a longer time horizon, the investor will make improvements to the property in an attempt to raise the property's value on the market. This kind of investment often requires a lot of hard work and may result in considerable financial outlays. A significant number of these investors will own just a single property at any one time.

6.2   Examine the state of your finances

Examine your portfolio. It is common practice to consider investing in real estate to be a portfolio enhancer, that is, an investment that supplements stock and bond holdings. When included into a bigger investing strategy, it has the potential to increase the predictability of your income.

6.2.1   Evaluate your assets

Conduct an inventory of your assets. Investing in real estate often requires a significant amount of cash, over and above the initial purchase price of the property. Consider if you have the financial means to maintain your investment even if the market swings against you.

- Due to the fact that real estate is a physical asset, it will be necessary to do maintenance and upkeep on it. Despite the fact that this is often funded by the rent that is paid by tenants, there may be periods when there are no tenants to occupy the property, in which case the expenses will fall upon the owner of the property.

Be aware of the fact that the cost of flipping a property may quickly add up. If you want to engage in the business of buying and selling real estate, you must always be ready for the worst-case scenario. In the year that it may take you to refurbish and sell your home, the real estate market might take a nosedive, leaving you with the burden of maintaining your mortgage payments while you wait for it to sell. Before committing to a potentially lengthy venture, check to see whether you have the financial means to do so. Before becoming engaged in home flipping, you should do research on the ins and outs of the process so that you may limit unanticipated costs.

6.3   Put a group together

Create a strategy. Decide where and how you want to invest your money. Consult with a financial advisor or an accountant before moving forward with your strategy. Discuss the strategy in detail with a financial planner. Check to ensure that nothing has been overlooked in this regard.

Acquire the ability to depend on the help of others. When it comes to making sure that everything goes off without a hitch during the whole process, a wise real estate investor will not be afraid to ask for assistance from other qualified specialists. Your level of investment will determine the composition of the team that you will need.

6.3.1   Learn to rely on other people

You could need the services of a mortgage broker, an accountant, a property manager, an attorney specializing in real estate, a house inspector, and an insurance broker. Enlist the assistance of an experienced real estate agent. If you are interested in real estate investment, it is in your best interest to work with a real estate agent that has prior expertise in the market for investment properties.

Find a real estate professional that can guide you through the process of looking for good investment homes. Conduct interviews with a number of different agents before settling on one. Talk about your objectives as well as your investing strategies. A skilled real estate agent will be able to show you homes that are suitable for the investment plan you have devised.

6.3.2   Talk to mortgage brokers

Talk to mortgage brokers. Your real estate agent ought to be able to provide you with recommendations for lending institutions. Have conversations regarding mortgage finance with the banks and credit unions in your area.

- Determine what the brokers, lenders, and banks have to offer in terms of the interest rates, closing charges, and payment arrangements that they can provide. Inquire about the several financing alternatives available to you, and choose the mortgage that corresponds most closely with your financial plan and investing approach.

Chapter 7

Step-by-Step Guide to Investing in Real Estate without Any Money

When you invest in residential real estate, you are getting more than just a house or a plot of land on which to construct a house when you make that investment. It is not unusual for people to purchase a home or piece of land with no intention of ever living there as a means of making money through the increasingly common practice of investing in real estate. Some investors don't do anything more than buy a piece of property and keep it in their portfolio while they wait for it to increase in value. The quickest and easiest way to enter the real estate market is to have cash available for a down payment, but this is not the only option available to you. A great number of people have discovered methods that allow them to begin investing in real estate with very little or even no money of their own. Borrowing money is one possibility; additionally, there are a number of other less conventional and original routes to ownership.

7.1   Investing without a Down Payment

Investigate the possibility of seller financing. If the seller is motivated enough, he or she may be willing to make it easier for you to purchase the property by providing you with a loan to cover the cost of the transaction. You could propose making larger payments on a monthly basis as an alternative to making a down payment.

- Another option you have is to arrange an agreement with the seller in which they pay your down payment to a conventional lender so that the property may be sold more quickly. You can be expected to pay the seller back, or the seller might just give you the down payment without expecting anything in return, thereby decreasing the selling price.
- To ensure that both parties are safeguarded, you should make sure that a licensed real estate attorney drafts the agreement for each of these potential scenarios.

7.1.1   Lease the property with the option to buy

You will have the chance to purchase the property if you lease it. You may ease into a real estate investment by signing a lease agreement and making payments on it until you have the funds to purchase the property outright. Your contributions would be used (at least partially) toward the total purchase price of the asset. Check that the agreement includes an explicit mention of the property's ultimate selling price. Determine the specific amount of each monthly rental payment that will be used toward the overall cost of the purchase.

7.1.2   Work out a trade

Make a deal for a trade. You may be able to acquire real estate by exchanging another piece of property or a talent that requires specific training on your part. For instance, a contractor may provide work to a real estate developer in return for a down payment if the developer was willing to pay the contractor.

- Other types of property, such as motor homes, campers, boats, automobiles, huge appliances, precious artwork, and furniture, might be part of a potential trade with you.
- Before engaging in any kind of bartering transaction, you should consult with a lawyer to draft a legally binding agreement that outlines the terms of the arrangement and specifies the value of each item being traded. It is possible that an impartial evaluation is required.

7.1.3 Take over mortgage payments

Take over mortgage payments. If you want to buy a piece of real estate but you don't have enough money for the down payment, you might make an offer to take over the mortgage payments in return for the right to the property. However, before you make such an offer, you will need to do research on the loan that is already in place. Certain types of mortgage loans have wording that expressly prohibits transactions of this kind.

- Instead of making a down payment, you may offer to take on the responsibility of the seller's other debts, such as their credit card bills. You might make payments toward this over a period of time. Put the arrangement in writing since, if you don't pay the credit cards on time, the seller's credit rating will suffer and it will be your responsibility to make sure this doesn't happen.

7.2   Co-Investing for a Down Payment

Bring along a friend or a companion. If you have a lot of great ideas but not a lot of money, finding a partner who will supply the finance while allowing you to handle the management of the project can be an appealing choice for you. You will need to draft a contract that defines who is liable for what and how the earnings will be split among the parties involved in the venture. If your partner is just there to provide financial assistance, it is essential that you continue to have complete and total control over the day-to-day operations of your venture.

7.2.1   Invest with a building contractor

Make a financial investment with a general contractor. Find a business partner who has the necessary skills to renovate and resell a home, such as carpentry, plumbing, and electrical work, if you do not possess these abilities yourself. This person should also be able to assist with the initial down payment. As soon as you turn a profit on the sale, you will have the funds necessary to make the first deposit on your subsequent real estate purchase.

7.3   Borrowing Money for a Down Payment

Take out a loan from your loved ones or close friends. If you want to make an investment in real estate but you don't have much cash on hand or any cash at all, another choice is to borrow money from close relatives and friends. Make sure that you draw out a formal promissory note that includes payment due dates, a specified interest rate, and the percentage of ownership that the lender will have in the property, if any. If you repay the loan on time and with the interest that was accrued, the lenders may be prepared to lend to you again for any more projects that you have in the future.

- You should think about the impact that not being able to repay the loan will have on your relationship with the financial institution that provided it. You should ask yourself whether the purchase of real estate is worth putting your connection with a person who is important to you at jeopardy.

7.3.1 Take out a home equity loan

Borrow against the equity in your house. You should look for a financial institution that would let you take out a loan for a down payment in addition to the mortgage loan you already have on your own home. This may take the form of an open line of credit or a second mortgage, both of which would use your property as collateral. You should look for a low interest rate that will enable you to buy the property at a price that is affordable enough for you to still earn a profit later on from the investment you made in it.

- Determine whether or not you will be able to repay this debt, or you run the danger of having your own house repossessed. In order to qualify for this kind of loan, you will need to have a credit score that falls somewhere in the upper 600s.

7.3.2 Consider a micro lender

Consider a micro lender. Internet micro lending services, often known as peer-to-peer lending, assist borrowers in locating lenders for relatively modest loans, typically those that are less than $35,000. Do some research on these websites and become yourself acquainted with all of the policies and procedures so that you can prevent confusion at a later time. Sites such as Kiva, Prosper, and Lending Club are examples of well-known micro lending platforms.

7.4 Finding Properties to Purchase

Engage the services of a seasoned real estate broker. Working with a real estate broker who is knowledgeable in locating houses that have the possibility of not needing a down payment won't cost you anything extra. You should go around to individuals who have expertise investing in real estate and ask them for the names of brokers they have dealt with. Check the website of the real estate firm for information on the background of a specific agent.

7.4.1 Seek out motivated sellers

Look for vendors who are highly motivated. These individuals are in a frantic state to sell their homes for a variety of reasons, including but not limited to personal bankruptcy, divorce, the death of a close family member, relocation for a new job out of town, the property's bad condition, falling behind on payments, and so on. They are going to be more willing to provide cash in order to fast seal the purchase. Your local real estate broker may be able to give you with information on other people who may be in a similar predicament.

7.4.2 Search online for properties that offer incentives

Do some research online to find rental homes that come with enticing extra? These may include financing from the seller with a low or even zero down payment. Check out homepath.com, a site dedicated to resale marketing. In addition to that, Fannie Mae provides listings for the hundreds of homes that it has acquired via the foreclosure process.

Chapter 8

Best REITs of the world

Investors have the option of protecting their portfolios against the effects of high inflation by purchasing real estate investment trusts (REITs). REITs are companies that hold real estate, and the value of the real estate they possess rises with overall inflation. In addition, the leases that are provided by real estate investment trusts are often designed in a way that makes it possible for the rent to be increased on a regular basis. It is expected that many of the most successful real estate investment trusts (REITs) for the remainder of 2022 will be those who have rent increases related to the consumer price index (CPI), which enables their revenue to keep pace with soaring inflation.

Nevertheless, this fall in sector values may provide an excellent opportunity for investors who are focused on income to stock up on dividends from wealthy REITs. The yield on the S&P 500 Real Estate sector is now at 2.5%, which is much higher than the yield on the S&P 500 Index, which is currently at 1.6%. In addition, there are a great number of high-quality REITs that provide yields that are higher than 2.5%, in addition to those that boast rapidly expanding dividends. Keeping this in mind, the following are the top REITs for the remaining years of 2022. These brands stand out from the crowd thanks to their high yields, dividends that are rising at a consistent rate, or outstanding resistance to the effects of inflation; in most instances, all three of these characteristics are present.

8.1　Rexford Industrial Realty

A rapidly expanding industrial warehouse real estate investment trust is Rexford Industrial Realty (REXR, $57.93 per share). In light of the ongoing difficulties in the supply chain, REXR has the potential to be one of the most advantageous REITs for the duration of 2022. Over sixty percent of the industrial real estate held by REITs is under Rexford's control in the region around the ports of Los Angeles and Long Beach. The firm does all of its business in Southern California, which has a huge industrial market worth $31.6 billion and is believed to be as big as the combined size of the next five largest industrial markets in the United States. According to Hoya Capital, the demand for industrial real estate is unquenchable as a result of interruptions in the supply chain and the expansion of online retail. 48 straight quarters of positive net warehouse space absorption is proof that despite record levels of new building, industrial warehouse space is still in short supply, and demand is strong.

This is shown by the fact that there have been record levels of new development. The performance of the Real Estate Investment Trust (REIT) during the March quarter was outstanding; core FFO per share increased by 29.7% year-over-year, and portfolio occupancy reached 99.3%. At the moment, the portfolio of Rexford comprises of 312 properties that have a combined total of 38.1 million square feet of rentable space. During the March quarter, the firm expanded its portfolio by purchasing 17 additional buildings and 1.5 million square feet of rentable space. Additionally, Rexford boosted its projection for 2022, stating that it expects core FFO per share increases of 13%

this year at the midpoint of its range. This is an increase from its prior view, which called for 9% growth. In addition, the REIT provided its shareholders with a substantial dividend increase of 31% earlier this year.

All eight Wall Street analysts who cover REXR give the company's stock either a Buy or a Strong Buy rating. REXR was selected as one of the top 10 stocks for 2022 by the analysts at Global Research, while Investor's Business Daily also recently included Rexford to its list of top-ranked growth companies that are exhibiting relative price strength and good fundamentals.

8.2 Sun Communities

Sun Communities is the biggest owner/operator of prefabricated home (MH) communities, recreational vehicle (RV) resorts, and marinas in the United States. Its stock price is now $151.04 per share. The real estate investment trust (REIT) is the owner of 646 properties spread out over Canada, the United Kingdom, and 39 states in the United States. Within the United Kingdom, its portfolio includes 283 residential communities, 192 recreational vehicle parks, 130 marinas, and 41 RV vacation sites.

Rent rises and occupancy improvements have been driving the REIT's organic growth in recent years. More than eighty percent of its mobile home parks have rental prices that are indexed to the CPI. During the March quarter, the company's manufactured home communities had an occupancy rate of 96.7% on average; however, approximately three-quarters of its sites exhibited 98%+ occupancy, which created extra upside potential connected to the remaining locations. The portfolio has almost quadrupled in size as a result of the property purchases that have totaled $11.1 billion over the previous decade. Internal growth has been enhanced as a result of these acquisitions. It is a REIT.

Additionally, it has an active development pipeline with the goal of bringing in three to five new development projects year. During the March quarter, UI's FFO per share increased by 6.3%, and the company's estimate for the full year projects increases of 11.5% at the midpoint in 2022. During the last quarter, Sun Communities successfully completed on acquisitions totaling $1.6 billion, including the purchase of 41 holiday parks in the United Kingdom and four marinas in the United States.

8.3　American Tower

American Tower (AMT, $234.49) is a prominent owner, operator, and developer of multi-tenant cell towers. It provides the infrastructure that drives wireless communications networks and is a market leader in this industry. The real estate investment trust works on a worldwide scale and is the owner of a portfolio that has 221,000 cell tower sites. Of these, there are 43,100 sites located in the United States, 49,000 sites located in Central and South America, and 75,500 sites.

Growing wireless penetration, rising consumption of mobile data, and spectrum auctions that make it possible to install additional antennas are all factors that are fueling the need for cell towers over the long run. The penetration of mobile devices is expected to expand at a pace of at least 10% each year until 2027, while the average amount of data used by each device is anticipated to climb at a rate of 21% per year.

The rise of the REIT may be attributed to the construction of more cell towers as well as the addition of new tenants to the properties it already owns. Return on investment (ROI) for an existing tower at AMT improves from 3% to 13% when a second tenant is added, and it jumps to 24% when a third tenant is added. American Tower has increased its dividend payment to shareholders on a quarterly basis since 2012, extending its streak of uninterrupted dividend increases to ten straight years. By REIT norms, a payout of 56% of adjusted FFO is considered to be cautious. Buy is the recommendation that was reached by the majority of the 20 market experts that followed the name AMT, which indicates that they believe AMT is one of the top REIT stocks for the remainder of 2022. AMT is currently rated as a Buy by the strategist at Citi, Scott Chronert, and the REIT was recently added to a list of quality stocks that Chronert has compiled and believes will outperform the market in the event that a recession occurs.

8.4   Prologis

The world's biggest owner of industrial real estate and a leader in global logistics, Prologis (PLD, $110.66) is a real estate investment trust (REIT). Its portfolio includes 4,675 commercial properties and more than one billion square feet of space available for lease. PLD is the owner of facilities in 19 different countries, with main supply-chain hubs located in North and South America, Europe, and Asia. The development of e-commerce has led to an insatiable demand for warehouse space, which the REIT capitalizes on to its profit as a significant participant in the retail logistics chain.

During the March quarter, PLD's portfolio had a retention rate of 75% and was leased out to 98% of its properties. The corporation was successful in raising rents by an average of 37% across the board. About 5,800 different clients are under Prologis's care, the most majority of them are involved in either business-to-business or retail fulfillment activities. The acquisition of REIT competitor Duke Realty (DRE) by Prologis for $26 billion is the biggest real estate transaction that has taken place since the epidemic started. Prologis is growing its footing aggressively. The areas of Southern California, New Jersey, South Florida, Chicago, Dallas, and Atlanta are among the most important markets in the United States, and Duke controls over 160 million square feet of warehouse space in these areas. It is anticipated that the transaction will be finalized during the third quarter of this year and will result in an immediate increase of 20 cents to 25 cents per share in core FFO.

When it comes to increasing dividends, Prologis is one of the top real estate investment trusts. Over the last decade, the corporation has boosted the amount it pays out to shareholders by roughly 11% every year on average. And Prologis maintains a payout ratio that is lower than 60% of adjusted FFO. In February, the real estate investment trust (REIT) presented investors with an increase in dividends that represented a 25% increase over the previous year.

8.5   The Digital Realty Trust

A large data center real estate investment trust known as Digital Realty Trust (DLR, $124.57) controls 291 facilities with a combined total of 35.8 million square feet of space spread out over 25 nations. Customers of DLR include cloud providers like Meta Platforms (META), IT companies like IBM and Oracle, mobile telecom companies like AT&T and Verizon (VZ), and LinkedIn. DLR's primary focus is on serving cloud providers, IT companies, and mobile telecoms.

A rapidly expanding digital economy as well as tailwinds associated with emerging technologies such as 5G, the Internet of Things, autonomous vehicles, and artificial intelligence are driving up demand for data storage and processing (AI). On an annualized basis, this REIT has produced growth in quarterly revenue for the past 12 consecutive years. During the quarter ending in March, year-over-year revenue increased by 3%, and record bookings were achieved by Digital Realty Trust. The growth rate of the FFO per share generated by the REIT was a respectable 6.7%. The ongoing demand for data center space, as well as the emergence of new lease opportunities, will drive future expansion. The occupancy percentage of the REIT's data centers is now at 83.3%, leaving potential for expansion. In addition, Digital Realty Trust is in the process of developing 8.1 million square feet of additional space for data centers and is holding onto 2.6 million square feet for potential future growth.

DLR was one of the companies that made it into BofA's list of top Alpha Surprise stocks. This list is a model that evaluates potential upside based on dividend discount and earnings surprise. Citi has included DLR shares on its list of strong growth firms that investors should consider purchasing amid pullbacks in the equities market.

8.6   Agree Realty Group Inc.

Triple-net-lease real estate investment trust Agree Realty (ADC, $67.00) primarily serves tenants in the e-commerce and other recession-resistant industries. Approximately 86 percent of the space owned by the REIT is leased out to major retailers, and 68 percent of those stores have investment-grade credit ratings. Tenants come from retail sectors that are resistant to the effects of a recession, including as grocery stores, pharmacies, home improvement stores, auto repair and tire shops, and convenience stores. These retailers include well-known brands such as Walmart (WMT), Kroger (KR), Lowe's (LOW), Tractor Supply (TSCO), and Dollar General (DG), among others.

The tenant in a triple net lease is liable for the expenses of real estate taxes, insurance, and property upkeep. Despite this responsibility, triple net leases are typically regarded to be less hazardous than other forms of leases. The business has a total of 1,510 properties located in 47 different states. These properties have a combined gross rentable area of 31 million square feet. In addition, the firm has 186 ground leases that have 4.9 million square feet of rentable space. Currently, the portfolio has a weighted average remaining lease term of 9.1 years and is leased out to a total of 99.6% of its properties.

Over the previous ten years, Agree Realty has increased its dividends by 5.5% on a yearly basis, on average. The most recent rise was 7.8% in the month of April, and the corporation started paying out dividends on a monthly basis in 2021. The payout ratio currently sits at a prudent 70% of the company's core FFO. Another reason why ADC is one of the best REITs for the rest of 2022 is that Moody's recently upgraded the company's credit rating to Baa1, recognizing Agrees low leverage and resilient portfolio. This is just one reason why ADC is one of the best REITs. Ronald Kamden, an analyst at Morgan Stanley, started covering ADC shares not long ago and assigned them an Overweight rating, which is equivalent to the word Buy. He likes the company because of its defensive qualities and the opportunities for growth it offers. In June, BofA analyst Joshua Dennerlein upgraded the stock to buy, citing defensive characteristics that should allow the real estate stock to outperform during a recession. These characteristics were cited as reasons for the upgrade.

8.7   W.P. Carey

W.P. Carey is a net-lease real estate investment trust (REIT) whose terms are tailored to keep up with the rate of inflation. Almost all of WPC's leases have built-in rent increases, with sixty percent of those increases being pegged to the rate of inflation. The majority of the company's single-tenant commercial real estate holdings are located in the United States and Europe. The company's current portfolio includes 1,336 buildings that may be classified as industrial, warehouse, office, retail, or self-storage facilities, totaling 157 million square feet of leased space.

There are more than 356 businesses now using the space that has been leased out. Some of the major tenants at W.P.

Carey include U-Haul, Advance Auto Parts (AAP), Extra Space Storage (EXR), Marriott (MAR), and the Hallway brand of German home improvement retail outlets. The portfolio has an impressive occupancy rate of 98.5% and a weighted average lease term of 10.8 years. W.P. Carey came to an agreement in February to purchase CPA: 18, a non-traded real estate investment trust (REIT) that the business was managing, for a total of $2.7 billion in cash and shares. W.P. Carey's foothold in the self-storage industry will be considerably enhanced as a result of this transaction, which is scheduled to be finalized during the third quarter and would position the company as one of the major owners of self-storage properties worldwide.

During the March quarter, W.P. Carey had an increase of 10.7% in its adjusted FFO per share. The REIT has projected that its adjusted FFO per share for 2022 would be 4.1% higher. The real estate company continues to be a favorite with Wall Street analysts, and according to S&P Global Market Intelligence, they have a consensus Buy rating for the stock. And thus far in 2022, two equities research companies, JMP Securities and Raymond James, have already commenced covering with Outperform (Buy) recommendations for the company in question.

8.8   National Retail Properties

One of the most reliable real estate investment trusts (REIT), National Retail Properties (NNN, $39.63), has raised its dividend payment every year for the past 32 years in a row. This established triple net lease is primarily for smaller properties located in the eastern half of the United States of America. At this time, the REIT owns 3,271 properties that are located in 48 different states and have a total of 33.5 million square feet of space that can be rented out. The portfolio is fully occupied with a weighted average lease term of 10.6 years and an occupancy rate of 99.2%. NNN's defensive strategy focuses on single-tenant, freestanding retail properties (no malls or strip centers) and tenants that provide low-cost essential goods or services that continue to do well during a recession. This strategy eliminates the need to compete with larger shopping centers. More than 370 retail businesses call National Retail Properties their home. Convenience stores, automotive services, and quick-service restaurants make up its largest retail sectors and account for a combined total of forty percent of the company's portfolio. 7-Eleven, Circle K, Goodyear (GT), Wendy's (WEN), Taco Bell, and Dave & Busters are among the tenants that have multiple locations (PLAY).

The REIT will typically acquire properties whose prices fall somewhere between $2 million and $4 million. A low initial investment results in more affordably priced rents for tenants, which not only contributes to the success of the tenants but also makes it easier to re-lease properties. During the March quarter, NNN completed the purchase of new properties worth a total of $210.8 million and sold 10 properties for a total of $20.1 million. The real estate investment trust has sufficient liquidity for further purchases. On the balance sheet for the March quarter, there was $53.7 million in cash, there were no amounts drawn on the company's $1.1 billion bank line of credit, and there were no significant debt maturities until 2024.

During the same time period, National Retail Properties experienced an increase of 11.6% in its core FFO per share during the March quarter. In addition to this, over the past five years, its core FFO has grown at a respectable annual average rate of 4.3%. The NNN stock price has decreased by 17.6% so far in 2022 due to the negative effects of broad-market headwinds. Despite this, Buy is the recommendation made by the vast majority of the 14 analysts that follow the REIT and whose work is monitored by S&P Global Market Intelligence. In addition, shares are now selling at an extremely advantageous valuation, as they are trading at a low 13 times future FFO, which is more than 8% below the median of the REIT industry.

8.9   Cube Smart

One of the top three most successful self-storage REITs in the United States is Cube Smart (CUBE, $38.87). It has 1,272 properties spread out across 154 different marketplaces and 38 different states in its portfolio. A further source of continually growing income for the corporation comes from the payments it receives to manage 664 properties that belong to other parties. Roughly 75% of the REIT's holdings are concentrated in the most in-demand metropolitan statistical areas (metropolitan statistical markets). Cube Smart is the uncontested leader in the market for self-storage facilities in New York City, which has a restricted supply of facilities and few new projects as a result of restrictive legislative changes.

Acquisitions, development, joint ventures, and the provision of management services by third parties have all contributed to CUBE's expansion throughout the years.

Since 2017, the REIT has successfully concluded acquisitions totaling over $3 billion, approximately $1 billion worth of joint ventures, and it has $92 million worth of new development projects in the queue. The transaction to buy Storage West was completed in December of last year and cost $1.7 billion. The purchase broadens the REIT's presence in desirable niche regions that are typified by high entry hurdles, including as San Diego, Orange County, Phoenix, Las Vegas, and Houston. Additionally, the transaction had an immediate positive impact on FFO. In the last five years, Cube Smart has seen an annual increase in FFO per share of 7.3% and an annual increase in dividends of 6.9% on average. During the March quarter, the REIT saw a rise of 23.1% in its FFO per share. Cube Smart has lots of flexibility for more mergers and acquisitions as well as development initiatives in 2022 thanks to its investment-grade credit rating and the absence of large debt obligations before 2024.

In June, CUBE received an upgrade to Strong Buy from Raymond James analyst Jonathon Hughes, who now considers this business to be his top selection among REITs. Hughes values the fact that self-storage REITs can mostly withstand economic downturns, and he believes that the better diversification that Cube Smart has across markets and tenants further decreases risk.

8.10   Essential Properties Realty Trust

Essential Properties Realty Trust is a net-lease REIT specializing in property sale-leaseback transactions for middle-market customers. Selling and leasing back their real estate to Essential Properties enables businesses to raise capital to reinvest their core operations. During periods of rising interest rates, sale-leasebacks are an attractive alternative to debt for companies in need of capital. At present the REIT's portfolio consists of 1,545 free-standing properties leased to 323 tenants across 46 states and representing 16 different industries. Its four largest tenant industries include early childhood education (14.1%), quick service restaurants (12.9%), car washes (11.5%) and medical/dental offices (11.4%). These recession-resistant tenants make up roughly 50% of the REIT's cash rents.

Essential Properties has grown adjusted FFO per share nearly 20%, on average, annually over three years and growth accelerated to 27% during the March quarter. The REIT is guiding for 13% FFO per share gains this year at the midpoint. Portfolio occupancy was nearly 100% during the March quarter and the portfolio's weighted average lease term is almost 14 years. EPRT acquired $238 million of new properties during the March quarter and envisions a growing M&A pipeline in 2022 due to more businesses seeking to monetize their real estate. The REIT has plenty of liquidity thanks to its investment-grade credit rating, no significant debt maturities before 2024 and a debt-to-EBITDA ratio among the lowest in the net lease sector.

The REIT has only paid dividends for three years, but in that time, it has rewarded investors with 34.4% average annual growth. EPRT most recently boosted its dividend in June, by 3.8%. Essential Properties earns Buy or Strong Buy ratings from nine of its 14 Wall Street analysts. Bulls cite the REIT's strong fundamentals and ability to benefit from rising interest rates via more demand for sale/leaseback transactions as reasons to invest.

Chapter 9

Basics of REIT Taxation

Investors who want to hold income-generating real estate but don't want the hassle of buying or managing individual properties often turn to real estate investment trusts, or REITs for short. Investors favor REITs because of the substantial revenue streams they provide. In order for the trust to be considered a REIT, it is required that at least 90 percent of its taxable revenue be distributed to the shareholders. As a result, real estate investment trusts are often exempt from paying any corporation income taxes since their profits are distributed to shareholders in the form of dividends.

Despite the fact that a consistent flow of payments may seem attractive, investors should be aware that REIT dividends come with their own set of particular tax repercussions. These payments may be considered taxable regular income, taxable capital gains, or a return of capital; the tax treatment for each of these scenarios would be different. In the following article, we will explain how real estate investment trusts (REITs) function and what investors need to know about the possible tax consequences of using REITs.

9.1   Fundamental Aspects of Real Estate Investment Trusts

A firm that owns, manages, or funds real estate that generates revenue is known as a real estate investment trust

(REIT). REITs operate in a manner that is similar to that of mutual funds in that they pool the money that is contributed by a large number of participants. After then, the funds are invested in various types of real estate, including but not limited to office buildings, residential complexes, retail malls, industrial estates, hotels, and resorts. With the help of real estate investment trusts (REITs), it is now feasible to invest in real estate without the difficulties that come along with property ownership, such as dealing with leases and maintaining the property. Each individual unit in a real estate investment trust (REIT) reflects a proportionate ownership stake in the REIT's underlying assets.

Real estate investment trusts are widely used as investment vehicles all over the globe. There are as many as 37 nations throughout the world where REITs may be purchased, and their total market value has topped $1.7 trillion. 2 In the United States of America, real estate investment trusts (REITs) are mandated to distribute at least ninety percent of their taxable income to their unit holders. 1 Because of this, real estate investment trusts (REITs) are appealing to investors who are looking for rates that are larger than those that can be received in conventional fixed-income markets.

9.2   Categories of REITs on the bases of tax

In general, REITs may be divided into the following three categories:

- **Equity REITs:** These trusts make investments in real estate and generate revenue via rent payments, dividends, and the selling of properties for a profit. This particular kind of REIT is quite common since it has three different sources of revenue.

- **Mortgage Real Estate Investment Trusts (REITs)** are trusts that invest their money in mortgages and mortgage-backed securities. Mortgage REITs are sensitive to fluctuations in interest rates since they get money from the assets in which they have invested.
- **Hybrid REITs** are a kind of real estate investment trust that invests in both mortgages and real estate.

9.3   Taxation at the Trust Level

A real estate investment trust (REIT) is a legal entity that, if not for its unique REIT structure, would be subject to the same taxation requirements as a corporation. For an organization to be considered a REIT, the majority of both its assets and its revenue must originate from real estate transactions. In addition to this, it is required to distribute ninety percent of its taxable revenue to its shareholders. Because of this condition, REITs do not normally have to pay taxes on their corporate profits; nonetheless, any retained earnings will be subject to taxation at the corporate level. A REIT has to have at least 75% of its assets invested in real estate and cash, and it needs to get at least 75% of its gross revenue from real estate-related sources like rent and mortgage interest.

9.4   Taxation to Unit holders

Investors in REITs may classify the dividend payments they receive as either regular income, gains in capital, or a return on their initial investment. All of this information will be broken out on the annual 1099-DIV that REITs send out to its shareholders. In general, the majority of the dividend is composed of money transferred to the shareholder from the real estate operations of the firm. As a result, this portion of the dividend is considered to be regular income by the investor. This portion of the payout is subject to taxation at the investor's highest possible rate of income taxation.

It's possible that the REIT may disclose to you that a portion of the dividend represents a gain or loss on the investment's capital. When the REIT sells property that it has owned for at least a year, this occurrence takes place. The capital gain or loss is likewise passed on to the investor; however, the investor's income level for the year in which the gain is received determines the rate of taxation that is applied to the gain, which may range from 0% to 20%.

In addition, a part of the dividend may be deducted as a return of capital, which is not subject to taxation. This may occur if the cash dividends from the REIT are more than the profitability of the REIT, for instance if the corporation incurs significant depreciation charges. There are two important points to keep in mind about a return of money. First, the unit holder does not have to pay taxes on this portion of the dividend in the same year that it was given to them. Two, the tax is not deducted till later. The cost basis of the unit holder is reduced whenever there is a return of capital. When the investor sells their units, this payout is subject to taxation as either a long-term or short-term capital gain or loss, depending on the circumstances. If the investor receives a sufficient amount of their original investment and the cost basis is reduced to zero, then any further non-dividend payments are subject to taxation as a capital gain.

Under the provisions of the Tax Cuts and Jobs Act, the taxable component of the REIT dividend that is attributable to income may be eligible for further favorable tax treatment (TCJA). The legislation introduces a new deduction of 20% for income from pass-through businesses, which may be used to eligible dividends from REITs. The deduction will no longer be available after the year 2025. It is important for those who do not live in the United States to be aware that the U.S. government may withhold thirty percent of their REIT income. If there is a tax treaty in place between the United States and the REIT holder's home country, the holder may be eligible for a lower tax rate as well as certain exemptions. An Example of the Tax Calculation for Unit holders an investor decides to purchase a REIT at the market price of $20 per unit. As a result of its business activities, the REIT earns $2 per unit, of which 90%, or $1.80, is distributed to unit holders. The profits contributed $1.20 to the total amount of the payout. The remaining $0.60 is considered a return of capital that is exempt from taxation since it is generated through depreciation and other costs.

The $1.20 gain would be subject to taxation in the investor's jurisdiction at ordinary income rates in the year that it was realized. In the meanwhile, the cost basis of the investor drops by $0.60, bringing it down to $19.40 per share. When the units are sold, the decrease in basis will be subject to taxation as either a long-term or short-term gain or loss, depending on which classification applies.

9.5   Crux of the Matter

Investors may benefit from REITs' one-of-a-kind tax benefits, which can translate into a consistent source of income for them, in addition to returns that are greater than what they might earn in fixed-income markets. However, investors have to be aware of the nature of these payments in order to determine whether they come in the form of income, capital gains, or a return of capital; this is because each of these categories is dealt with in a distinct manner throughout the tax filing process. Additionally, qualifying dividends from REITs may be eligible for extra tax benefits under the TCJA5. Investors should speak with their own personal financial advisors to have a better understanding of how REIT dividends may affect their tax liabilities. This is due to the fact that everyone's tax circumstances are unique.

Chapter 10

Pros and Cons of REIT's

Investors in equity real estate trusts have the opportunity to acquire commercial real estate without being responsible for its management. REITs buy and are responsible for managing commercial real estate via the use of competent management teams. If you buy shares in a real estate investment trust (REIT), you will eventually become a co-owner of the properties it manages. When seen from this angle, you are also a part-owner of an active company that provides property management services in exchange for compensation. Although the majority of REITs are publicly listed on major stock exchanges, a few REITs are privately owned and follow the structure of mutual funds.

The term "REIT" refers to real estate investment trusts, which may own a broad variety of assets, including but not limited to retail malls, hotels, manufacturing facilities, and student accommodation on the campuses of large universities. They almost always recruit the most capable management teams. The team's responsibility is to manage the properties in order to achieve the highest possible profits and rental revenue. At the corporate level, equity REITs are not subject to taxation.

10.1   Advantages of REITs

10.1.1 Property Management

Through the use of REITs, even the typical investor may own commercial property. Additionally, the investor gets the advantages of having expert property managers strive to create money for them without the typical problems that are associated with being an ordinary landlord. The marketing, the collecting of rent, the administration of tenants, and the upkeep of the facilities are all handled by a management team that has been carefully chosen. The only thing required of investors in REITs is to receive their dividends.

10.1.2 Returns through Dividends

When it comes to equity equities, management has the option of either distributing dividends to shareholders or reinvesting earnings in the business. On the other hand, real estate investment trusts (REITs) distribute at least 90 percent of their income to their shareholders. The decision of what to do with dividends is then left up to the investors. When investors decide to put their money back into the market, they do so by purchasing more shares. They are free to do anything they choose with their dividends, including spending the money on a trip if that is what they would like. The amount and number of dividends paid out is typically stable, although REITs provide the potential for additional payouts in the event that rents go up. Appreciation is also attainable via realizing the increasing value of the assets held in the trust, which is another method.

10.1.3 Returns through Appreciation

REITs have traditionally fared well owing to the consistent long-term appreciation of commercial real estate, despite the fact that you won't experience the degree of price hikes that you would with equities companies in a favorable market. Share prices of equities stocks and commercial real estate investment trusts (REITs) are often more susceptible to the short-term effects of changes in inflation and interest rates than are prices of commercial real estate and REITs. Investing in bonds may result in fair returns with an acceptable level of risk; however, the prices of the majority of bond classes are fixed, and there is little possibility for appreciation.

10.1.4 Low Volatility and Low Correlation

The price volatility of REIT shares is much lower than that of equities stocks. Because of this, both short-term and long-term projections of rental revenue and administration expenditures may be reliably made. Because rental revenue is often extremely predictable, it is easier for analysts to forecast the performance of real estate investment trusts (REITs) than they are able to forecast the performance of equities companies. Predictions made by analysts on the performance of REITs have a good chance of being correct. This results in a decrease in the share price's volatility.

Additionally, there is a minimal connection between the success of REITs and the performance of other asset types. This indicates that their behavior is not often comparable to that of bonds or equities securities. Because the performance of their share prices is mostly unrelated to that of equities stocks and other investment classes, including them in a diversified investment portfolio may be beneficial. Real estate investment trusts (REITs) often perform better in times of falling stock prices, which helps to keep the performance of your portfolio in check.

10.1.5 Diversify Your Investment Portfolio

When you start investing in real estate investment trusts (REITs), you'll have the chance to diversify your investment portfolio. You may reduce the amount of risk and uncertainty associated with your portfolio by diversifying into other asset classes, such as real estate, in addition to bonds and stocks. Additionally, real estate has a positive connection with stock prices, which shields your investment from the gyrations of the market. As an investor, you may rapidly diversify your portfolio in the real estate market by purchasing stakes in a variety of properties located in a number of different industries. It's possible for investors to take a very modest sum of money and distribute it among a number of different property types, such as commercial buildings, industrial warehouses, and residential complexes. Such funds, in most circumstances, consist of large assets such as hotels or office buildings, which some investors are unable to access.

Additionally, REITs provide you the opportunity to diversify your portfolio regionally. They make it possible for you to acquire a portion of the ownership of properties located in a variety of nations, states, and localities. Foreign investors, who are often prevented from owning properties in another nation, are able to purchase ownership interests in real estate investment trusts (REITs).

10.1.6 Access to commercial real estate

Another benefit of REITs is that they let you to put your money to work in commercial real estate assets, which is beneficial if you are interested in investing in commercial real estate. In most cases, a large number of individuals are unable to acquire a class an office building on their own. You may own a piece of hundreds of different types of real estate, including retail malls, housing complexes, and data centers, if you invest in REITs.

10.2   Disadvantages of REITs

REITs are subject to a number of the same risks that are associated with investing in equities. These are the most important drawbacks associated with investing in real estate investment trusts.

10.2.1 Weak Growth

REITs that are traded on a stock market often distribute a significant amount of their profits to shareholders and other investors. Regrettably, there is not a lot of money left over that may be used by a REIT to expand its holdings. Private REITs, on the other hand, are not subject to the same regulations and, as a result, may be able to keep more of their revenues for further investment.

10.2.2 High Rates of Taxation Placed on Dividends

When compared to dividends received from other investments, those received from real estate investment trusts (REITs) are subject to a higher tax rate. Dividends are the only kind of income that are typically subject to a tax on capital gains. However, REIT returns do not qualify for the lower rate; rather, they are subject to the rates that apply to regular income. Obviously, this is heavily influenced by the nation in which you now reside.

10.2.3 Potentially High Fees and Risk

Even though a real estate investment trust (REIT) is registered with the SEC, this does not indicate that it is risk-free. Before investing in real estate investment trusts (REITs), potential investors should give careful consideration to a variety of aspects, including interest rates, the real estate market, tax legislation, location, and more.

10.2.4 Trends Affect the Performance of REITs

In comparison to other types of investments, real estate investment trusts (REITs) are more susceptible to the ups and downs of the real estate market. For instance, if a REIT has a major investment in rental buildings in an area where rental revenue is declining, the returns for shareholders are likely to trend downwards. This is because rental income is a direct reflection of the region. Since real estate is the only investment destination for REITs, avoiding fluctuations in that market presents a greater challenge than for other types of investment vehicles.

10.2.5 Little Control over Performance

People who invest in physical properties have a greater degree of control over their investments, which is one of the REIT Advantages and Disadvantages that works in their favor. If you invest your own money, you have the ability to cherry-pick properties with high returns, market empty rental spaces aggressively, and meticulously evaluate applicants for rental agreements in order to maximize income and reduce risk. You now have a far greater degree of control over the manner in which you put real estate best practices into action.

If, on the other hand, you choose to put your money into a real estate investment trust (REIT), you won't have any control over how well that investment does. If you are unhappy with the returns it generates, your only practical choice is to sell it. Another disadvantage is that some private real estate investment trusts do not let you to sell your shares for a number of years after you have purchased them.

10.2.6 Implications for Taxes

Because real estate investment trusts are considered pass-through businesses, they are seldom subject to taxation at the corporation level. It's possible that this will change depending on the nation in where the investments are being made. Having said that, this is pretty much the norm in every single region in the planet. Simply adding the dividend income produced from REITs to the individual's other sources of income is all that is required. This implies that investors in REITs may be subject to a tax liability of up to 37% on the income that they have generated as a result of their investment in certain circumstances. As a result, income from REITs is subject to taxation at a more onerous rate than that applicable to income from other assets, like as equities, which are subject to taxation at a more advantageous rate.

10.2.7 Confined by Time

The asset class of real estate is considered to be illiquid. Because of this, investors are unable to liquidate their real estate investments nearly as rapidly as they can sell other asset types, such as stocks or bonds. This issue is precipitated by the very high monetary worth of the assets held in real estate. REITs are also affected by the same issue. REITs have a finite lifespan. This indicates that the REIT management is obligated to liquidate the property at the conclusion of a certain time period (let's say ten years), at which point the returns are to be distributed to the owners of the investment. As a result of the fact that numerous REITs reach their maturity at the same time, this might put downward pressure on pricing. There is also the possibility that REITs may be required to sell their assets at a period in which values are falling.

When real estate investment trusts reach their maturity stage, new investors often step in to purchase the properties that were previously held by older investors. Nevertheless, as prices fall, it becomes difficult to recruit new investors, and the properties really have to be sold in order to liquidate money and pay off the investors who were previously owed money.

Conclusion

Let's recap:

Real Estate Investment Trust is what "REIT" stands for in the industry. A real estate investment trust (REIT) is a partnership, company, trust, or association that invests directly in real estate by purchasing buildings or mortgages. REITs may be established as either for-profit or nonprofit organizations. Shares of a REIT are issued, traded on the stock market, and purchased and sold in the same manner as regular equities. A corporation must invest at least 75% of its total assets in real estate and generate at least 75% of its total revenues from real estate-related operations in order to qualify as a real estate investment trust, often known as a REIT. As early as 1960, the federal government opened the door for investors to participate in large-scale commercial real estate developments by making it feasible for them to do so. However, private investors have just begun to show interest in REITs in the last ten years.

Low interest rates, which forced investors to look beyond bonds for income-producing investments, the advent of exchange-traded and mutual funds focusing on real estate, and, prior to the real estate meltdown of 2007-2008, an insatiable appetite on the part of Americans to own real estate and other tangible assets are some of the reasons for this trend. As was the case with almost every other kind of investment in 2008, REITs experienced significant losses. In spite of this, they remain to be a valuable asset that should be included in every diversified investment portfolio.

Real estate has long been acknowledged as a historically important investment class, potentially offering increased portfolio diversification, low volatility, and superior risk-adjusted returns. REITs make it easy to not just invest in real estate, but to instantly invest in a *multitude* of real estate assets through the simple purchase of a single REIT's shares. While not all REITs are easy to access or particularly affordable, many are. Thanks to that accessibility, a REIT can often present the most appealing route for an individual to become a real estate investor.

Ultimately, it's up to each investor to determine their own circumstances and personal preferences. For instance, some investors will find that the financial and regulatory restrictions of fully private REITs present no problems, and they might consider the upsides of private REITs to be worthwhile. For many other investors, open accessibility and affordability will make public REITs — either traded or non-traded — the clear choice. And finally, for many investors, new alternatives like Fund rise's eREITs may prove to be the most compelling option. Whatever your experience is as an investor, there's a good chance that there's a REIT investment option suitable for you.

Investors may benefit from REITs' one-of-a-kind tax benefits, which can translate into a consistent source of income for them, in addition to returns that are greater than what they might earn in fixed-income markets. However, investors have to be aware of the nature of these payments in order to determine whether they come in the form of income, capital gains, or a return of capital; this is because each of these categories is dealt with in a distinct manner throughout the tax filing process. Additionally, qualifying dividends from REITs may be eligible for extra tax reductions under the TCJA. 5 Investors should speak with their own personal financial advisors to have a better understanding of how REIT dividends may affect their tax liabilities. This is due to the fact that everyone's tax circumstances are unique. There is no other evidence that adequately demonstrates the relative security of making investments in the real estate market. There is a consensus among industry observers that the current pace of home price appreciation is unsustainable. On the other hand, even in the event that there is a correction, it is possible that it will have minimal impact on the performance of real estate investments in the long term. There is a general agreement among financial experts that real estate investment trusts (REITs) make for a strong long-term investment, in spite of the fact that they are susceptible to considerable fluctuations in the short term. If you want to invest but want to avoid the volatility of the stock market, real estate investment trusts (REITs) are the appropriate investment instrument for you.

That said, I urge you to complement what you've learned here with some research of your own to iron out the kinks based on your specific location and regulations that may impact your projects. I hope this book has been useful, and I hope I've provided you with the tools to make an informed decision about what is, potentially, a worthwhile investment.